THE
PLYMOUTH TO TURNCHAPEL RAILWAY
(and The Cattewater Goods Line)

by
Anthony R. Kingdom

ARK PUBLICATIONS (RAILWAYS)

First published in 1996 by ARK PUBLICATIONS (RAILWAYS), an imprint of
FOREST PUBLISHING, Woodstock, Liverton, Newton Abbot, Devon TQ12 6JJ

British Library Cataloguing in Publication Data
A catalogue record for this book is available from the British Library
ISBN 1–873029–03–9

Class 02, No. 233, and train crosses the swing bridge over Hooe Lake on 14th June 1926.
H. C. Casserley

ARK PUBLICATIONS (RAILWAYS)
Editorial and design by:
Mike Lang

Typeset by:
Carnaby Typesetting, Torquay, Devon TQ1 1EG

Printed and bound in Great Britain by:
BPC Wheatons Ltd, Exeter, Devon EX2 8RP

Cover photographs:

Front — (Top)   Plymouth, Friary Station during early SR days with the Turnchapel
train on the extreme right of the picture. Class 02 No. 233 is in
charge.

Lens of Sutton

(Lower)   Class 02, No. 233, with an Adams chimney, crosses Hooe Lake
with its two-coach train on 14th June 1926.

H. C. Casserley

Back –   Class 02, No. S 182, still carrying its SR number, entering
Turnchapel Station on 23rd June 1949.

S. C. Nash

CONTENTS

ACKNOWLEDGEMENTS

The author wishes to extend his grateful thanks to the following for their generous assistance, given in a wide variety of ways during the preparation of this book:

Associated Portland Cement Co./Blue Circle Industries plc; Bayley Bartlett Ltd; British Rail, Records Office, Kew/British Railways Board; Central Electricity Generating Board; The Historical Signalling Society; *Mid Week Independent*; Plymouth City Council (Planning); Plymouth City Library; Plymouth Joint Services Transport; Plymouth Railway Circle; *South Devon Times*; South Western Gas Board/British Gas S. W.; West of England Fishing & Ship Co.; *Western Evening Herald*; *Western Morning News*.

R. Bragg; L. Crosier; A. Edwards; H. Elford; W. French; B. Gibson; R. Harding; P. Hesseltine; D. Holland; H. Hutton; B. Kohring; P. Lucas; J. Nicholas; P. Powell; E. R. Shepherd; W. E. Stevens; L. Summers; R. Taylor; G. Wright; M. Wyatt.

(*A number of photographs have been kindly lent, and these receive individual acknowledgement in the captions*)

PREFACE

The fore-runner to this book, *The Turnchapel Branch*, was published in 1982 by the Oxford Publishing Company which, just beforehand, had passed into the ownership of Blandford Press, an imprint of Link House Group plc of Poole, Dorset. However, by Christmas 1985, the title had already been remaindered and made available to 'bargain' bookshops with the result that its value as an historical document was seriously impaired

During 1987 the O.P.C. again came under new ownership, this time becoming part of the Haynes Publishing Group of Sparkford, Somerset, and in July of that year I was requested to enter into a new agreement with this company. Whether any residual stock was then held is a matter of conjecture, but suffice to say my hopes of seeing the title reprinted, sadly, went unfulfilled.

Now, some 14 years after the original book was published, I am delighted to have had the opportunity to update the work, as well as include some new material that has recently come to light in the possession of the Plym Valley Railway, and to present it to the proprietors of Forest Publishing for publication under its new title *The Plymouth to Turnchapel Railway*.

The Publisher and I feel confident that this updated reprint will delight those who were unable to obtain a copy of the original book. In doing so, we hope to have given pleasure to those interested in this essentially urban part of Devon's railway history.

Anthony R. Kingdom
Thalassa
Newton Ferrers
Devon
March 1996

INTRODUCTION

The Southern Railway branch line from Plymouth to Turnchapel was only $2^{1}/_{2}$ miles long and when I began to write a history of the line I thought that only a very small book would result, even if I included the goods line known as the Cattewater Branch, with which the Turnchapel Branch was intimately connected because of their geographic positions. However, it is surprising how much information is still available about such small branch lines as these, which formed such a complex network over the country during the late 19th and early 20th centuries, and which are in their way just as much a part of railway history as the more famous, larger lines.

The Turnchapel Branch had a history of only 64 years, but the portion of the line from Plymouth Friary to Plymstock and the Cattewater Branch are still open to goods traffic, totalling 89 years to date. Neither line had any great claim to scenic beauty, but their existence altered for all time the face of that part of the estuary of the River Plym which is known as Cattewater. Industry flourished on the western bank of the estuary, where the Cattewater Branch ran, whilst on the eastern bank the two villages of Turnchapel and Oreston developed to such an extent that they are now suburbs of the City of Plymouth. At the turn of the century these two villages were served by rail and sea, but by the early 1920s they were also served by road transport. By the late 1960s only the road transport remained and now, with the railway closed and the steamers gone, only the number 7 bus route of the 'Plymouth Joint Services' remains.

The transport by rail of cement and liquid petroleum gas still sustains the Friary to Plymstock section, while oil and bitumen are the main goods carried on the Cattewater Branch. During these uncertain days of recession one may only speculate as to the probability of their survival into the 1990s.

Anthony R. Kingdom
June 1982

THE TURNCHAPEL BRANCH — A Description of the Route

The Turnchapel Branch was 2½ miles long, commencing at the former London & South Western Railway terminus of Plymouth Friary. The main Up and Down lines connected Friary with the GWR system at Friary Junction, some 74 chains to the east of the station. From there all trains to the main LSWR system enjoyed running rights over GWR metals via Mount Gould Junction, Lipson Junction, Mutley and North Road Stations before regaining their company's own metals at Devonport Junction, 43 chains west of North Road Station.

A further line emerged from the complex layout at Friary, adjacent to Friary 'B' Signal Box and ran parallel to the Up and Down main lines for a considerable distance. Commencing as No. 1 road, it became the Down siding. It connected with the Motive Power Depot to the east of the station and also to the Cattewater/Turnchapel branch line further to the east, which passed the MPD before swinging southwards in a large curve to Cattewater Junction.

However, before we embark on the journey to Turnchapel, the grandeur and complexity of the former LSWR's main terminus at Plymouth Friary at its zenith must be described. It was a large railway complex, almost wholly self-contained, with the passenger and goods sections built on the site of an old Friary whence the name was derived. This place was an ideal situation for a main line terminus since it was positioned adjacent to the city centre and its main shopping area.

The layout of Friary Station consisted of the following: (a) The passenger terminus with all the main and branch line facilities for passengers and their welfare. (b) A goods station lying further to the south with all the freight-handling facilities including excellent road/rail access. (c) A Motive Power Depot approximately half a mile to the east with its coaling, water and loco-turning facilities.

The passenger and freight stations lay in a triangle bounded by Beaumont Road and Knighton Road to the north, Friary Gate to the west and Exeter Street, St. Jude's Road and Desborough Road to the south. The entire lay-out was bisected roughly NW to SE by an impressive, multi-arched limestone bridge carrying Tothill Road to the south on its journey to Cattedown from Greenbank and Mutley Plain.

The main entrance to the passenger station was from either the western or eastern ends of a slip road off Beaumont Road on to which the main station building faced. A rear entrance at the SW corner of the main platforms gave direct access to Exeter Street via steps.

On the Upside lay the main station building, constructed in a grand manner, its design functional yet elegant, its proportions impressively spacious. The overall appearance was of a long, single-storey building constructed of rough blue limestone, with its corners, doorways, roof edging and window-sills of a dressed stone of lighter colouring, probably white limestone. A matching set of very much smaller buildings stood on the Down side, which were purely functional and for staff use. Returning to the main building, the window frames and doors on the road side were of heavy timber and most windows had the rounded apex design to the top fanlights which employed the use of four small panes. A lateral stepped dressing was given to the entire length of the building at window-top level, the whole appearance echoing that of an Abbey or Friary such as the one which had existed there centuries before.

The gabled roof, which was in three sections, was covered in Welsh slate, the centre or main section sporting four small dormer windows. The roof was furnished with two quadruple flue chimneys of matching limestone situated on its end sections, whilst the centre of the middle section reached a climax in an ornamental spire and weather vane. Triangular vents with trefoil-shaped apertures punctuated the remainder of the length of the roof. Entry to the building was under a large canopy supported on two ornate cast iron legs which held aloft a triple-apex, glass-panelled roof structure.

Passengers approaching under the canopy and entering the main booking hall would, after purchasing their tickets, emerge on to the Up platform. The Up and Down platforms were joined at both the western and eastern ends. A short end platform bridged them at the western end whilst their centres were connected by a covered footbridge. The latter was constructed of a latticed steel framework, the risers of the stairs being masked from the open ends of the platforms by matching stonework. All but the extreme eastern ends of the platforms were covered by large spacious canopies supported upon their own girders which rested upon larger longitudinal spans of latticed girderwork. These in turn were supported by large round cast-iron pillars set off with ornate wrought iron cornices.

Six terminal tracks entered the station from the eastern end; these were the Up and Down main roads, with a centre road for empty coaching stock, the Up and Down bay roads for branch line traffic and a short additional Up bay road. The latter was popularly known as the scenery dock, because it was from here that the scenery for the Palace and other local theatres used to arrive and depart with its respective touring company. Through the large double gates to the roadway outside, animals and stores for the touring circuses emerged and were then marshalled for the usual parade through the town en route to their local site.

The layout of the station buildings and their functions, together with the wartime alterations, can best be described with the aid of the sketch opposite.

The goods shed consisted of a large red-brick structure, 300 ft. long by 100 ft. wide, lying some 50 ft. to the south of the eastern end of the passenger station. The side walls were finished with a dozen alcoves in which much smaller multi-paned steel windows were inserted. The roof of matching Welsh slate ended at the iron rainwater guttering with an

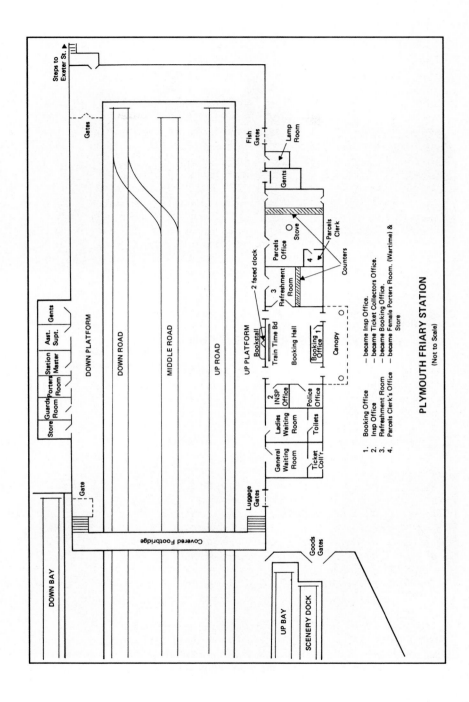

PLYMOUTH FRIARY STATION
(Not to Scale)

1. Booking Office — became Insp Office.
2. Insp Office — became Ticket Collectors Office.
3. Refreshment Room — became Booking Office.
4. Parcels Clerk's Office — became Female Porters Room. (Wartime) & Store

7

The main entrance to Friary Station c1949.

W. E. Stevens

Friary Station from the road bridge – early 1950s.

L.G.R.P.

Three Class M7s stand at the eastern end of Friary Motive Power Depot during June 1954.

Photomatic Ltd.

intermittent facia of the decorated ends of the main supporting beams, while the apex of the roof was totally glazed for additional light. Two sidings ran through the goods shed to buffer stops at Friary Gate. Four sidings of varying lengths lay on its southern side whilst two more lay to the north.

The LSWR Friary Branch ran parallel to the above sidings but lost height rapidly as it dropped into a deepening cutting and passed under Exeter Street by means of a short tunnel. This branch reappeared east of Sutton Road and crossing it by means of a level crossing, ran down to North Quay to join up with the Sutton Harbour Tramways. It also connected west of Coxside Gate with the GWR North Quay Branch which was a secondary line off the GWR Sutton Harbour Branch from Friary Junction.

Finally, four sidings, one equipped with a crane, lay to the south of the Friary branch cutting, and this was known as the Mileage Yard. A private road commencing at Friary Gate and serving the goods station from Exeter Street ran around the westward end of the passenger station to join with the slip roads in from Beaumont Road.

About a half a mile to the east of the passenger and goods stations was the Motive Power Depot with some ten sidings in all, three running through the engine shed. This building was constructed of red brick and measured approximately 320 ft. long and 60 ft. wide. Between each pair of wall piers were installed large thirty-paned window frames to maximise the available daylight. The roof was of slate with a louvred smoke outlet vent running the entire length of the roof ridge. This was supplemented by a number of square venting chimneys running along both sides of the middle roof sections. The ends of the building were open with the gable ends completely glazed. During the early 1950s the square chimneys were removed and the glazed end sections replaced by corrugated iron sheeting. Coaling and watering facilities were situated to the eastern end of the depot, i.e. the coaling shed in the south-east with rising 'hump' from yard level, whilst behind stood the main water-tower. The water cranes supplied by the tower stood outside the shed ends, and to the north-east of the tower was located the turntable.

If we return in imagination to the passenger station, a typical journey to Turnchapel may now be described. The period used for this nostalgic exercise will be during the very early 1950s, just before closure to passenger traffic. An ex-LSWR Class O2 and two 'gate type' suburban coaches await the 'off' in the Up bay or number four road of Plymouth Friary Station. The 'Up bay starter' signal drops and the train starts away, heading east to pick up the 'Up main' line after first passing Friary 'B' Signal Box. Negotiating the northernmost arch of Tothill Road Bridge, the train gathers speed as the rear of 'Friary 'B' to bay road inner home' is passed. At this point the main lines and their accompanying sidings on the southern side run below Knighton Road. At the end of Egerton Place, the

'Friary 'A' to branch home' and Friary 'A' Signal Box, (where the Friary 'A' to Cattewater Junction tablet is obtained) are passed in quick succession. Knighton Road and Desborough Road run parallel to the railway, to the north and south respectively.

Eastwards from here the train crosses from the 'Up main' line, over the 'Down main' line to join up with the Cattewater/Turnchapel Branch line, over pointwork which also gives access to Friary Motive Power Depot south of this point. It was from here the mile posts measured the distance to Turnchapel.

On a rising gradient, the single line climbs above the two main lines which now stretch eastward like four silver threads. Gaining height still, the view from the train widens considerably. To the north lies the green expanse of Tothill Park bordered by Lanhydrock Road in the foreground. Behind lie a profusion of geometric rows of terraced houses, built about the turn of the century, forming the residential area of St. Jude's. Further to the north stretches the panoramic view of Greenbank and Mount Gould areas each with their large hospital buildings. To the south of the line the train is passing Friary MPD complex with 'Friary 'A' to branch starter' and 'Cattewater Junction Down distant' standing adjacent to the left of the line opposite the locomotive turntable. Immediately afterwards, the train slows, passing the rear of 'Friary 'A' from branch home' as it eases to rest at Lucas Terrace Halt.

The Halt, at MP ¼. opened in 1905, consisted of a long concrete platform which was lengthened by 125 feet during the mid-1923 rebuilding. Its entire length was of stone and earth infill with concrete slab edging to a loose chippings surface. It was situated on an embankment well above the main lines to the north, thus giving its access to the south a steep incline for passengers to negotiate. To the south also were Lucas and Stenlake Terraces which led out to Embankment Road. A narrow underpass running below both the branch and the main lines carried Lucas Terrace out to join up with Lanhydrock Road to the north. (This was closed to motor traffic in more recent years).

On the platform stood a small precast concrete shelter with a tiled roof and windows at each end. The rear of the platform was bordered by a concrete post and wire fence, and a steep path with wooden handrails led down to Lucas Terrace from the eastern end of the shelter.

Departing from Lucas Terrace Halt, the train swings away southwards on a severe curve, making the wheel flanges squeal in protest, as it continues over a latticed girder bridge passing over the double tracks of the GWR Sutton Harbour Branch on its way to and from Friary Junction. In addition, the 4ft. 6in. gauge track of the horse-drawn Lee Moor Tramway runs parallel to the Sutton Harbour Branch, passing under the bridge en route from Lee Moor Clayworks to Martins Wharf.

The Turnchapel train continues to sweep around to the south passing the rear of 'Cattewater Junction to Friary starter' and the 'Cattewater

Two views of Lucas Terrace Halt during March 1968. a) Looking westwards towards Friary; b) Looking eastwards towards Cattewater Junction. In the background can be seen the Lanhydrock Road overbridge, Friary Junction with the main lines to Friary Station, the GWR's Sutton Harbour Branch (closed December 1975) and the LSWR bridge over it.

Author

West Country Class No. 34001, running light on the triangle at Cattewater Junction on 23rd June 1949. Such locomotives were too large for Friary turntable so were turned in this way. The locomotive is standing upon the branch line and in the background can be seen Lanhydrock Road Bridge and Friary Junction Signal Box, whilst curving away to the left are the SR main lines (one obscured by the bank).

S. C. Nash

Lucas Terrace Halt c1949.
L.G.R.P.

Two views of Cattewater Junction in 1960 showing a) The signal box and original level-crossing gates for the track to Martins Wharf; b) in 1970 showing a mixed goods train leaving the Cattewater Branch and the newer level-crossing gates for a track crossing, then disused.

Author's Collection & W. E. Stevens

Junction Down home' signals just prior to crossing the Embankment (Road). The latter is crossed by means of another latticed girder bridge of matching design. With the bridge over the Embankment left behind, the twin tracks of the GWR Yealmpton Branch approach the train on the left side on their way to and from Mount Gould Junction. They had crossed the Embankment some 50 yards further to the east over their own bridge. Here is Cattewater Junction and the meeting point for both the Cattewater/Turnchapel and the Yealmpton branches. Cattewater Junction Signal Box, where the tablet is exchanged for the next section to Plymstock, is passed at MP ½ to the right of the train as it continues on its journey south.

Leaving Cattewater Junction, and passing the rear of 'Cattewater Junction to Friary Up home', the point is encountered where the common line divides into the Cattewater and the Turnchapel branches. Here the Cattewater goods branch continues southwards to pass under Laira Bridge Road, past Prince Rock ground frame, to emerge on to Corporation Wharf and ultimately on to Cattedown Wharf adjacent to the Cattewater itself, thus traversing the western bank of the estuary of the River Plym.

The Turnchapel Branch, however, climbs on to a short embankment and turns eastwards to cross the River Plym, passing 'Cattewater Junction Down starter', 'Plymstock Down fixed distant' and MP ¾ on its way. The River Plym is spanned by the now familiar pattern LSWR lattice girder bridge. This one is constructed in six sections, the ends of each of the six spans butted together in five pairs of cross-braced, tubular steel legs. The west and east ends rest on limestone-faced abutments to their respective embankments. The train crosses at a steady 15 to 20 mph allowing passengers more than a glimpse of the wide and varied views both up and down stream from this point.

Looking upstream on the eastern bank is Skentlebury's boat-yard, and further upstream are the more sylvan settings of Chelson Meadow and Saltram Park, the latter's boathouse nestling against the waters edge. Saltram House itself can just be seen from here, particularly during the stark and leafless winter months, whilst away in the distance can be seen the southern fringe of Dartmoor, no matter the season. There the contrast of the green-brown moor with the off-white claypits of Lee Moor is unique.

Saltram House, (now owned by the National Trust), was erected in the 18th century by Lady Parker. The estate was owned at the time by Sir James Bagge, vice-admiral of Devon and Cornwall, whose avarice and rapacity earned him the nickname 'Bottomless Bagge'. Towards the end of the 18th century, John Parker became Baron Boringdon from the name of his old family seat at Plympton and in 1815 his son became the first Earl of Morley. The latter distinguished himself both as an engineer and a business man, he reclaimed a portion of the Laira (Lower Plym) and extended the grounds of Saltram Park. This he did by building an embankment to keep out the waters of the Plym and draining the reclaimed land. He also built the famous Iron Bridge over the Plym on the southern side of the estate. This ran adjacent to the railway but preceded it by many years and was the only road exit from Plymouth to Plymstock and the South Hams until replaced in recent years.

Returning to the exhilarating views northwards from the train, on the western bank of the river past Cattewater and Mount Gould Junctions, lie the complex trackwork of Laira Motive Power Depot belonging to the former GWR. This is flanked on the south side by the main line in and out of Friary. Running in from further west to impinge upon the northern flank are the GWR main lines to and from Plymouth North Road Station.

At a point further north where the GWR main lines run in from Plympton past the depot, they hugged the river bank passing Blagdon's boat-yard which was as far as the eye could see.

Downstream from the railway bridge across the Plym, a more industrial view meets the gaze of the train's passengers. Looking past the adjacent iron road bridge carrying the A379 to Kingsbridge and the South Hams, the western bank of the river is overshadowed by the two sets of chimneys of the power stations. The taller brick chimneys are of the newer oil-fired power station opened in the early 1950s, the smaller are the steel tubes of the 1898 coal-fired power station built to supply current to Plymouth trams. Crowding along the confines of Corporation and Sutton Wharves are many and varied industries ranging from oil and fertiliser to scrap iron. Behind and in the distance is the additional light industry of Cattedown with its oil terminal, tar distillery, acid works, chemical manure works, oxygen works, gas works and abattoir. This is the land of the Cattewater Branch from which our line recently diverged.

Downstream on the eastern bank of the river are the scrap yards of Davies and Cann, and the builder's yard of Curtis & Co. Further downstream, past the mouth of Pomphlett Lake, are the waterside communities of Oreston and Turnchapel, separated by Hooe Lake which is tidal from the Cattewater. These former villages are the *raison d'etre* for the branch itself although still 1½ miles away by rail. Finally the backcloth to this residential and industrial scene is the radio masts of Staddon Heights, the eastern landmark of Plymouth Sound.

After crossing the River Plym, the train crosses the Ride, or entry into Chelson Meadow and Saltram Estate, by means of a short steel bridge. Here, almost opposite the 'Morley Arms' on the road below, the train passes the rear of 'Cattewater Junction to Up Friary distant' signal as it negotiates a short embankment at MP 1 below Pomphlett Quarry. The train continues past 'Plymstock to Turnchapel home' signal, the site of the original signal box and the rear of 'Plymstock Up main starter'. The latter shares a gantry with the 'Up starter' of the Yealmpton Branch at the apex end of the station platform.

The Turnchapel train leaves the bridge over the River Plym en route for Cattewater Junction and Friary during the summer of 1950.

W. E. Stevens

Plymstock Station, looking west on 28th August 1960. In the background can be seen the chimneys of Plymouth's 'A' & 'B' power stations and the corporation destructor.

M. Hale

Plymstock Station viewed on a journey in the 1950s was a mere shadow of its former self, having been damaged by enemy action during 1941. The platforms however remained intact, their construction being similar to that of Lucas Terrace Halt. The two platforms for Turnchapel and Yealmpton formed a 'V' or triangular configuration, joining at their western end towards Plymouth. The original station was built in typical Victorian style but of an austere corrugated iron sheeting for the walls and roof. It contained a gents' toilet, ladies' room, booking hall, booking office, station master's office and goods and parcels office. To offset the austerity of the walls and roof there was a wooden facia with perforations in the design of 'triangular bats', alternately reversed, ending at each apex with tall finials. The GWR platform sported a rather more ornate canopy of vertical wooden planking with glazed end panels to offer protection from the wind. The LSWR platform was devoid of any covering to protect its passengers, although there was nothing to stop them using the other platform. It did however, possess a set of five beautiful twisted spiral, cast-iron lamp standards standing on cylindrical bases. Their oil-burning lamps were housed in the most elegant copper lanters, perhaps more suited to Friary Station than here.

The original signal box was of LSWR design and stood to the right of the line just prior to Plymstock Junction. It was closed during July 1935 and a new frame opened in the booking office to replace it. This of course was destroyed in 1941 and another new box was opened in October of that year. The sight that would meet the eye of a prospective passenger during the post-war years was what could only be described as a 'motley collection of hutments'! The best of these was a replacement signal box of green and white lateral wooden planking with eight four-panelled windows along the Yealmpton platform side and at each end. This was built on to a four-panelled concrete slab construction covered with corrugated asbestos giving a 'garden shed' appearance, and formed the booking office at the rear of the signal box. To the west of the signal box stood another building of precast concrete slab construction, with rusty metal windows, which was the replacement goods shed. Between the two stood a very small ladies' and gents' toilet building constructed in a similar fashion to the signal box.

Other adornments to the station were precast concrete fencing, precast concrete lamp and telegraph posts with the Southern Railway 'bar and quadrant' support for the single filament lamp and its reflector. These supported the station name signs in green and white 'circle and bar' design of British Railways, Southern Region.

Various wooden telegraph poles carrying up to four arms, and a permanent way hut on the site of the original signal box were the only non-concrete items to be found. Despite the austerity of the original station, this appearance in the 1950s was indeed a mere shadow of its former self.

To return to our imaginary train journey down the line: leaving Plymstock Station the train heads in a southerly direction passing the slate-fronted former station master's house set back from the line, the 'Plymstock Down main starter' and 'Turnchapel Down fixed distant' signals, just prior to crossing No. 1 bridge spanning the A379, Billacombe Road. The rear of 'Plymstock Up main home' signal is sighted on the far side of the bridge as the train heads out on to a long high embankment towards Oreston. It was from Plymstock Station that both over and under bridges were numbered by the Southern Railway for identification purposes rather than employing geographical locations.

The next major bridge on the branch to be negotiated is No. 4, constructed of limestone and carrying the line over Pomphlett Road adjacent to Stamps Corner, but before reaching this place, during progress along the embankment, the train has to cross over four minor bridges. The first two, Nos. 1a and 1b, are, in fact, sluices allowing the ebb and flow of water from the high reaches of Pomphlett Lake. Following these are two underpasses into Pomphlett Mill Quarry, Nos. 2 and 3. All are of limestone construction but only the shoulders of No. 2 can be seen from the train.

Views from the train on this embankment include, to the west of Pomphlett Lake with the old corn mills at its head, Oreston Road running parallel to the line below and on its far side, Bedford Quarry. To the east lies Mill Pond, an extension of Pomphlett Lake with Pomphlett Mill (Moore's) Quarries adjacent to its southern flank. Just before bridge No. 4 over Pomphlett Road we pass MP 1¼ and as the train passes over the bridge the back gardens of Millway Place come into view. Following these, No. 5 bridge carrying the road in from Oreston to Honcray is reached, as Oreston Road swings away westwards at right angles to the line. The embankment has now given way to a deep cutting as the train passes below the bridge and all views are obscured. Breaking out of the cutting on to a long low embankment at the rear of Longlands Road, the train sweeps around in a gentle curve westwards as MP 1½ and Oreston Station are reached.

Oreston Station is little more than a halt, half a mile from Plymstock, and has one platform 160 ft. long and similar in construction to that of the stations described previously. It has one building constructed of vertical planking covered with asbestos sheeting supporting a small canopy over the doorway to the waiting room. Two large windows are situated one at each end of the building, one at the southern end in the former booking office and one at the northern end in the former goods shed/office. Two lamp standards carrying the usual lamps and electricity supply wires stand on the platform as does the station nameboard, all of course on concrete posts. A small two-lever ground frame at the northern end of the station allows entry into the eleven-waggon private siding and loading dock of F. J. Moore Ltd., situated at the rear of the passenger platform. At this end also is a 'barrow crossing' over the line connecting a footpath to

A view of the track over Stamp's Bridge adjacent to Oreston Road on a very wet day during the late 1950s.

W. E. Stevens

POMPHLETT HOUSING ADJOINS THE BUSY COMMERCIAL SCENE BESIDE RIVER PLYM

The area on each side of Billacombe-road can easily remain a mystery to travellers in and out of Plymouth. This week's aerial picture shows the housing development (foreground) on Pleasure Hill. The thoroughfare on the left, from the railway bridge, is the western end of Pomphlett-road, and those leading off it are Reigate-road and Howard-road. Between Pleasure Hill and the now-disused railway are the stonecrete works of F. J. Moore, Ltd., beside Mill Pond. On the right are the tall buildings of Associated Portland Cement Manufacturers, Ltd., by Pomphlett Quarry. The new dual carriageway section of Billacombe-road runs between new works sites alongside Pomphlett Lake to the fine new Laira Bridge (top), which straddles the River Plym, with Plymouth on the far side. On the left of Pomphlett Lake are Bedford and Breakwater Quarries.

An aerial view of the Pomphlett area taken in 1962 shows the following:–

A) Cattewater Junction Signal Box; B) Plymstock Station; C) Stamp's Bridge; D) Yealmpton Railway track-bed; E) Billacombe Road Bridge; F) Billacombe Road.

Western Morning News Ltd

A Class B4 with a short goods for Turnchapel has just crossed Stamps Bridge cJune 1954.

R. C. Sambourne

Class B4 No. 30088 runs light to Plymstock en route for Friary c1954.

R. C. Sambourne

Oreston Station showing F. J. Moore's private siding and loading dock, looking towards Turnchapel c1950s.

W. E. Stevens

Oreston Station after closure to passengers, looking towards Plymstock.
Lens of Sutton

Bridge No. 6 during the early 1950s, showing the road into Oreston Station and the rear of Turnchapel Up fixed distant signal.

W. E. Stevens

The departure of Bayly's siding at Bridge No. 7, with its two-lever ground frame controlled by Annetts key from Plymstock Signal Box.

W. E. Stevens

BR diesel No. 11228 leaving the branch at Bayly's siding with a timber train.
July 1952.

W. E. Stevens

BR diesel No. 11227 on a railchair train at Bayly's during 1950. These railchairs were made by G.K.N. Ltd. and fitted to the wooden sleepers on site.

W. E. Stevens

Truckloads of railchairs being unloaded at Bayly's. Further truckloads of new timber can be seen on the quayside behind.

W. E. Stevens

Bayly's timber yards with a train of empties headed by BR diesel No. 11234.

W. E. Stevens

the six railway cottages belonging to the railway which still house their employees.

Facing the stationary train from here is another long cutting extending from Houldsworth Road to the rear of Broad Park. Spanning the cutting just south of Oreston Station is bridge No. 6 carrying Plymstock Road over the line. To the right of the track stands the rear of 'Plymstock Up fixed sitant' signal, mounted on a latticed metal post.

Emerging from the cutting and heading in a south westerly direction, we pass MP 1¾ followed closely by Radford Crossing. This is a footpath crossing leading in from Oreston through the allotment gardens to the west. It crosses the line, passes Radford Cottages and runs into Radford Quarry adjacent to the shores of Hooe Lake. Warning of approaching trains is given by the operation of trembler bells by the train leaving Plymstock Station. The train, still running in a south westerly direction passes below the disused Langshill Quarry and crosses an underpass into the quarry by means of bridge No. 7. Immediately afterwards, the facing points are controlled by Annetts Key from Plymstock Signal Box, and allow access to Bayly's timber yards. Here the Turnchapel Branch line divides into two, and the passenger branch continues forward but a short goods line diverges to the left of the track, dropping on a fairly steep gradient to sweep in an arc and pass under the passenger line at bridge No. 8, some 8½ chains further on.

Bayly's timber yards were situated on the north side of the entry from the Cattewater into Hooe Lake. Here railway sleepers were treated with creosote as were power and telegraph poles and all types of timber for building. At the junction with Bayly's siding stood the 'Turnchapel Down home' signal beckoning the train to its journey's end. From here the line ran out on to a short stub embankment, and on to the unique bridge No. 9. This was a manually-operated swing bridge mounted on a single support with two sets of latticed run-outs either side of the entrance to Hooe Lake. Dolphins stood in the waters below to protect the supports from damage by shipping. It was opened after being released by Turnchapel Signal Box, by the signalman walking on to it and hand-cranking the mechanism. Here he would remain until the bridge was closed again and he was marooned no longer.

Once clear of the swing bridge the train entered Turnchapel Station in a westerly direction passing the replacement signal box and the rear of 'Turnchapel Up starter' signal. Although Turnchapel Station was the terminus for passenger trains, the line continued on to Admiralty Wharves for goods trains.

The original Turnchapel Station was also destroyed by enemy action early in the war, when nearby oil tanks were bombed and set alight. The blazing oil ran down on to the station and signal box, destroying both. There was one platform 175 ft. in length constructed in the same manner as the others on the branch except that the platform edge was lined with a

Three views of the swing bridge across Hooe Lake during the summer of 1959. a) In close-up looking towards Turnchapel Station; b) in the process of opening; c) open for a modern yacht.

W. E. Stevens

A general view of the Hooe Lake Bridge during the mid 1950s, looking out to the River Plym from Hooe Lake. The C.E.G.B. power stations can be seen on the far bank of the river in the background.

W. E. Stevens

The 1941 replacement signal box, complete with closure notice, at Turnchapel during early 1951.

W. E. Stevens

Class 02, No. S 182, still carrying its SR number, on the 12.48 pm ex-Friary train entering Turnchapel on the 23rd June 1949.

S. C. Nash

Turnchapel Station c late 1950s.

W. E. Stevens

'soldier course' of bricks. Entry was by a path and a steep flight of steps off its northern end leading out on to Undercliff Road, below the swing bridge.

The solitary station building was identical to that at Oreston except it had no goods shed end, just the booking office and waiting room. Two lamp standards stood either side of the station building and a large bank rose steeply at the rear of the platform.

The track layout at Turnchapel was a running line and loop with three sidings into the oil depot on its southern side. The original signal box was of LSWR design and constructed of timber with an apex roof. Long windows extended for one side and some two thirds of each end.

The post-war buildings that passengers on our train would see, were much the same as those at Plymstock Station with the signal box position transferred to the opposite side of the line. Both the replacement booking office/waiting room building and the signal box were of lateral wooden planking and asbestos sheeting and concrete slab construction, and were poor replacements to the original station.

As already stated, the line continued on for approximately 500 yards in a north-westerly direction from Turnchapel Station, for goods trains to Turnchapel Wharves. The line first went through a short steep cutting, before entering a tunnel under the houses of Boringdon Road to emerge on to Admiralty property. As the line emerged at the other end it diverged into double tracks which continued to curve around in a tight arc ending up travelling in an easterly direction to the wharves themselves. A reverse siding ran southwards back from the running line, over a crossover on the second line, to serve two storage areas within the complex.

The wharves were originally constructed to deal with goods traffic for Messrs. Bulteel but were taken over by the Admiralty during World War One and remained in its custody ever since. Their use today are for the mooring and repair of their cableships. Stores and spares are kept on the site as well as oil fuel tanks but activity here during the 1950s is much less than during the periods of World Wars One and Two.

County Maps of the Plymouth to Turnchapel Line. c1914 & 1933.

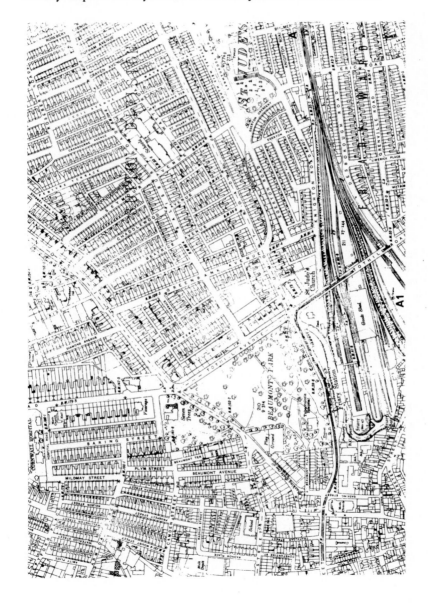

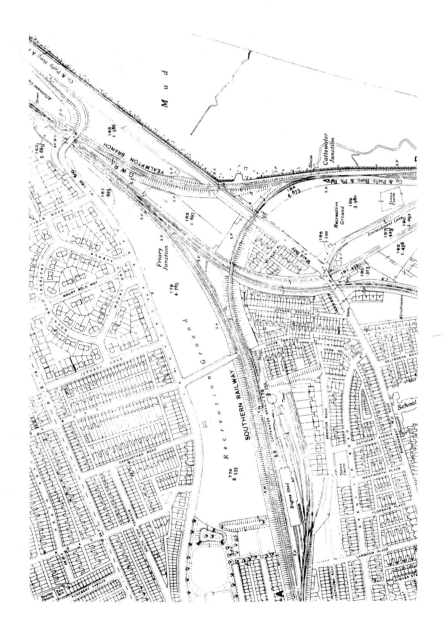

Cattewater Branch Terminus (Reduced scale).

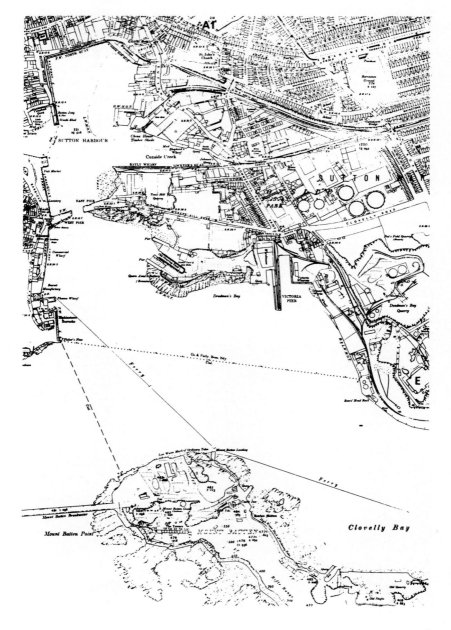

THE CATTEWATER BRANCH – A Description of the Route

This branch cannot be described as a scenic route despite its proximity to the River Plym. It ran through the most intense commercial dockland to be found anywhere in Devon. Because of its commercial nature and the ever-changing world of the demands of commerce, it naturally changed its layout much during its lifetime. During the 1950s, about the time of the described trip over the Turnchapel Branch, the Cattewater Branch was very busy indeed. After its divergence from the Turnchapel Branch just south of Cattewater Junction, it ran down the northern bank of the River Plym directly opposite Oreston and Turnchapel on the southern bank, and was often in view from the Turnchapel train.

The complex network of sidings existed to serve the CEGB generating stations and the various activities of Corporation Wharf. From here, its divergence into two routes took the shape of a flattened circle. The southern route hugged the river bank and served Cattedown Wharves, with their excellent handling and storage facilities for all goods coming in by sea. The northern route swung inland to serve the abattoir and meat market, passing under Cattedown Road by means of the 48-yard-long Cattewater Tunnel, and swinging south again to reunite itself with the southern route, running out on to Esso Wharf as dual track. From here still clinging to the Cattewater, it turned northwards adjacent to Esso Wharf Road, past the oil storage depots and tar distillery, and headed for Victoria Wharves.

Meanwhile, a spur ran north east via a level-crossing to Deadman's Quarry. Finally, at the end of the line near Victoria Pier, the line served the large oil storage and loading depots of the Conoco and Esso Companies, together with the coal yard and coal loading and storage facilities. This point was two miles and nineteen chains from Friary.

The western end of the 48 yard long Cattewater Tunnel taken from the former Fisons depot sidings. 1st May 1981.

36

Author

A selection of photographs taken on the Cattewater Branch during 1st May 1981, showing BR Class 08 No. 08 659 a) at Maxwell Road level-crossing with Propane/Butane wagons for the Shell depot, b) shunting in the Conoco oil terminal with diesel oil and bitumen wagons for Esso, and c) on the level-crossing at Cattedown Road with empties from the Shell depot.

Author

THE TURNCHAPEL BRANCH —
A Short History

Conception by the Plymouth & Dartmoor Railway Company and
Opening by L S W R

Extracts from Minutes of Plymouth & Dartmoor Railway Co.
1886 — 1896

Meeting of the Directors held at 32 Great George Street
Thursday 24 June 1886

Present

Mr. John W Batten in the Chair
Mr. Jas B Batten
Mr. A C White
In Attendance
Mr. A O Scott, Solicitor

Letter having been read dated 18th June 1886 from Messrs. Relf and
Pethick relative to Contract for making the junction with the existing
Line to junction of Modbury Line Act 1883 and 1884 — one third —
part of Railway No 1 of 1882 and 1883 length 5 furlongs 1 chain
including the Bridge over the Laira. It was resolved that the Chairman be
authorised to negotiate Contract with Messrs. Relf & Pethick for the construction of this portion of Railway and the Bridge as mentioned above on
the basis of the payment of £26,000 — being made in Cattewater
Extension Shares of the Company.

Resolved that as the powers of taking lands compulsory expire on the 1st
August 1886 the Engineers to be requested to prepare Land Plans and the
Solicitors to negotiate for the purchase of the lands required for the Bridge
and portion of the Railway as mentioned above and that notices to treat
be prepared.

Meeting of Directors held at 22 Great Winchester Street on
Tuesday 10th August 1886

Present

Mr. James B Batten in the Chair
Mr. Arnold de Beer
Mr. A Cromwell White

Secretary reported that the seal of the Company has been affixed to the
following; viz:-

Contract with Messrs. Relf and Pethick for construction of part
of works authorised by the Act of 1883.

Meeting of Directors held at 22 Great Winchester Street EC
Friday 26th August 1892

Present

Mr. John W Batten in the Chair
Mr. A C White
In Attendance
Mr. David S Derry, Secretary

Secretary reported correspondence with the Board of Trade, giving
notice July 15 1892, that the portion of Railway No 1 including the
Bridge over the Laira, had been adapted for Passenger traffic, and is
ready for inspection.

Meeting of Directors held at 32 Great George Street on
Saturday 11th February 1893

Present

Mr. J W Batten
Mr. A C White
Mr. Jas B Batten

Solicitor having reported that the Agreement with Mr. Pethick for the
construction of the Company's Railway from Plymstock Station to
Turnchapel had been finally settled between Mr. Pethick and the local
Committee, and that Mr. Pethick had sealed the Agreement, it was
resolved that the seal of the Company be affixed to the Agreement in
duplicate.

Meeting of Directors held at 22 Great Winchester Street EC
Friday 8th November 1895

Present

Mr. John W Batten in the Chair
Mr. James B Batten
Mr. Thomas Bulteel
Mr. A C White
In Attendance
Mr. David S Derry, Secretary

Letter dated 21st September 1895 from Mr. Lewis Sparrow stating that he had exceeded his Contract price £3,000 for excavations in Turnchapel extension by £1,294 7s 6d and asking for consideration of the Board thereon.

Letter dated 17th October 1895 from London and South Western Railway was read advising the Company that the plan showing the proposed connection and signalling etc at Plymstock has been approved by the Directors and that Mr. Fisher the District Engineer at Exeter had been instructed to at once confer with Mr. Masterton as to the work being proceeded with.

Letter dated 22nd October 1895 from the Board of Trade in reply to Secretary's letter of the 18th inst, was read, with regard to their requirements in opening the Turnchapel Branch of this Company's Line.

Meeting of Directors held at 22 Great Winchester Street EC
Wednesday 17th June 1896

Present

Mr. J W Batten in the Chair
Mr. James B Batten
Mr. Thomas Bulteel
Mr. A C White
In Attendance
Mr. D S Derry

Letter was read dated 22nd May 1896 from Board of Trade enclosing copy of the report made to them by Col. Addison of his inspection of the Turnchapel Branch of this Company's Railway.

Meeting of Directors held at 22 Great Winchester Street on
Friday 24th July 1896

Present

Mr. J W Batten in the Chair
Mr. J B Batten
Mr. A C White
In Attendance
Mr. D S Derry, Secretary

Letter was read from the Board of Trade dated 22nd July postponing the opening of the Turnchapel Line for one Calendar Month.

Meeting of Directors held at 22 Great Winchester Street
Wednesday 11th November 1896

Present

Mr. John W Batten in the Chair
Mr. James B Batten
Mr. Alfred C White
In Attendance
Mr. David S Derry, Secretary

Secretary reports that the seal of the Company was affixed to the following:-

Undertaking that the single line of Railway between Plymstock and Turnchapel shall be worked by the Electric Tablet system.

Before further consideration is given to the early history of the branch line from Plymouth Friary to Turnchapel, the development of the railways in South Devon should be recorded as a useful introduction.

In 1883 the Plymouth, Devonport and South Western Junction Railway Company was formed and on 2nd June 1890 opened a new line from Lydford into Devonport, Kings Road via Tavistock and Bere Alston. Despite being owned by the smaller company the line was worked by the London & South Western Railway and it completed the final link to their independent line from Exeter to Plymouth, or rather to Devonport.

The original realisation of one of the hopes and aspirations of the champions of the LSWR had been its initial entry into Plymouth on 17th May 1876. This followed the arrival of the Okehampton Railway (later the Devon & Cornwall Railway) at Lydford, which the broad gauge of the Launceston & South Devon branch of the South Devon Railway had reached during 1862. In 1866 the SDR had been given powers to convert the Launceston & South Devon branch to mixed gauge. A junction had been considered as early as 1874 but it was not until 1876 that the SDR had actually laid the additional standard gauge track allowing mixed gauge traffic over its route to Plymouth. At the same time the LSWR constructed a line from a point west of the triangle outside Millbay Station, on the main line to Cornwall, to connect with its new station at Devonport, Kings Road.

A new, through station at North Road was jointly conceived by both the SDR and LSWR to coincide with the working of through trains from Lydford. It opened on 28th March 1877 and was of course some ten months late for its intention.

Meanwhile the LSWR, via the Devon & Cornwall Railway agreement with the South Devon Railway, had constructed a goods station at Friary

Green as early as 1878. It opened for goods traffic on 1st February of that year. (It seemed as though the LSWR was anticipating the receipt and despatch of through passenger trains over its new independent route, right into Plymouth). However, to reach Friary from Devonport, the LSWR were still dependent on the former SDR line through Plymouth which was absorbed by the GWR in 1876.

The GWR opened the Lipson Junction to Mount Gould curve on 1st April 1891 which gave them direct access to Sutton Harbour. (This Sutton Harbour Branch of the GWR was double tracked). A year later, on 1st July 1892, the LSWR opened Plymouth Friary to passenger traffic, running their trains directly from Exeter over their route north of Dartmoor. Their negotiated running rights over the now GWR main line through Plymouth from Devonport Junction to Lipson Junction were supplemented by further rights over the curve between Lipson Junction and Mount Gould Junction and thence departing from the 'direct access' Sutton Harbour line at Friary Junction.

Having thus established their new passenger station terminus very close to the heart of Plymouth, the LSWR set about the consolidation of their position and looked towards the South Hams. By now the existence of the Plymouth & Dartmoor Company was drawing to its close, even as a spearhead for the London & South Western Railway. One of the last efforts of the P&D was to deposit plans on 30th November 1882 for a short branch to Turnchapel and Clovelly Bay. The Act of Parliament became law on 2nd August 1883 and the first step to railway access over the agriculturally rich area of the South Hams was thus taken. Turnchapel and Oreston themselves were not in the South Hams but to reach these two villages meant the construction of a bridge over the River Plym adjacent to the existing 'Iron Road Bridge'. The potential of such a bridge was quickly realised and on 30th November 1883 further plans were deposited for another line leaving the Turnchapel Branch at Plymstock to Yealmpton and Modbury. In fact, only the part as far as Yealmpton was ever built, eventually opening on 15th January 1898. (See the history of *The Yealmpton Branch*, Oxford Publishing Company 1974).

The new railway bridge across the River Plym was duly constructed and was completed by 1887 but the shorter Pomphlett Branch (to Plymstock Station) including the bridge, did not open until 5th September 1892. The official opening took place on 1st July 1892 but public trains were not immediately permitted until certain signalling standards were improved. Meanwhile the LSWR and P&DR were in conflict with the GWR over the Yealmpton to Modbury route. The LSWR finally gave way conceding the Plymstock to Yealmpton section to the GWR in an agreement of 19th July 1894. The LSWR having lost the initiative were not interested in pursuing the Yealmpton to Modbury section and were left with only the Turnchapel branch to construct.

The part of the line from Plymstock to Turnchapel was opened on 1st

Photograph taken about 1900 from the bridge over the double tracks of the Yealmpton Branch between Mount Gould Junction and Cattewater Junction. On the centre line of the scene, from left to right are:– Cattewater Junction Signal Box; the GWR and LSWR bridges over Embankment Road; the LSWR bridge over the GWR Sutton Harbour Branch and Lee Moor Tramway. The LSWR bridges carried the Turnchapel/Cattewater branches.

J. B. N. Ashford

A nearly new swing bridge over Hooe Lake opens for the 'John Nathaniel Rowse' on 1st October 1896.

Courtesy L. Summers

July 1897 and trains ran from Friary. The following year, on 15th January 1898, the GWR commenced the train service to Yealmpton using return running rights over the section from Cattewater Junction to Plymstock.

During the late 1890s and early 1900s the growth of housing development in the eastern suburbs of Plymouth was accelerating. In 1905 the LSWR opened a halt at Lucas Terrace to help serve this new populace. It must be remembered that there was strong competition for passengers to Oreston and Turnchapel, and from a waterborne source at that! In 1871 the Oreston and Turnchapel Steamboat Company had been launched, the brainchild of the late Mr. H. Elford. Four steamboats (the Greyhound, Beagle, Lightning and Eclipse) ran a ferry service from Phoenix Wharf near the Barbican to serve these two villages. Ten years later, in 1889, these boats were replaced with four new ones bearing the names Swift, Rapid, Lively and Dart.

Furthermore, the *Western Daily Mercury* for 25th July 1887 covered details of a new pier opening at Turnchapel. It had cost Mr. Elford £1,200 to erect the pier measuring 182 ft. long by 8 ft. 6 in. wide, and the contractors were Messrs. Lapthorne and Gould of Plymouth. It is on record that this service claimed some 10,000 passengers per day on Bank Holidays, all at 1d per head!

Following the opening of Lucas Terrace Halt in 1905, the LSWR opened its new Motive Power Depot on land adjacent to the rear of the halt during 1908. The original Motive Power Depot adjacent to Friary Goods Station closed at the same time.

World War One brought much increased traffic to the line, for the Admiralty took over the wharves at Clovelly Bay, Turnchapel. (They have remained in Admiralty hands to this day although truncated from the national rail network since 1963). Supplies for the Royal Navy including fuel and heavy engineering stores were stored at the wharves. Accordingly passenger traffic was supplemented by the maintenance staff and others who worked at this depot. After the cessation of hostilities, the naval depot continued to stimulate goods traffic on the line adding to the more general traffic existing.

History of the Turnchapel Branch as part of the Southern Railway

It was during 1923/4 that the many railways of Britain were regrouped into four main companies and the Turnchapel Branch became part of the new Southern Railway.

On the passenger side, the growth during the post-war years of the population at the eastern end of Plymouth stimulated traffic in and out of the town centre. To accommodate the longer trains required to satisfy the increased traffic, the platform at Lucas Terrace Halt was extended by 120 ft. during 1923.

The 1920s indeed proved to be the halcyon days of many of the railway branch lines, too early to be eclipsed by the motor car, which for many years to come was financially out of reach of many families; the Turnchapel Branch was no exception despite new competition by road as well as by sea. From 1923 to 1927 the Devon Motor Transport Co. ran bus services to Plymstock from Plymouth and it is believed these were extended as far as Hooe Lake. Further road competition to the train services arrived in 1928 when no less than three companies were running bus services to Hooe from Plymouth. They were 'Palace Saloons'; 'Eddystone Motors'; and 'Hopper & Berryman's'. In March 1929 the latter took over 'Eddystone Motors' and became 'H. B. Buses' whilst in May 1929 the 'Palace Saloons' were taken over by the newly formed 'Western National Omnibus Co.'. In 1930 'H. B. Buses' reformed into the 'Southern General Omnibus Co. Ltd.' and later, in November 1931, the 'Western National' took over the 'Southern General'.

The landing stage at Turnchapel as seen on an old postcard dated c1908.
Author

45

Two studies of the ferry service to Oreston and Turnchapel during the first world war Period: a) the 'Rapid' at Oreston Quay, b) the 'Swift' arriving at Turnchapel pier.

Courtesy R. Lang

Turnchapel Pier during the 1950s showing the 'Swift' and the 'Lively'.
W. E. Stevens

A later picture of the 'Rapid' beached for repair during the 1950s. A notice-
able difference in this later picture is the construction of a forward wheel
house in the bow of the ship.

Courtesy R. Lang

Two studies of Friary Yard, east of the station, during early SR days:–
Above: Looking towards Lucas Terrace Halt and the Branch with the houses
of Knighton Road clearly visible to the north.

Lens of Sutton

Below: Looking towards the overbridge and Friary Station. In the foreground
is the North Quay and Sutton Harbour line dropping away to the tunnel under
Exeter Street.

Author

A Class 02 No. 225 and one coach train from Turnchapel is the arrival on the Down road at Friary during the 1930s.

Lens of Sutton

The Turnchapel train headed by Class 02 No. 207 near Friary Motive Power Depot on 22nd May 1935.

H. C. Casserley

Class 02 No. 177 still in LSWR livery on 18th July 1924, heading the Turnchapel train past Friary shed.

H. C. Casserley

A view westwards from Lucas Terrace Halt in Southern days, showing the branch and main lines to Friary.

Author

This superb and original study of Lucas Terrace Halt shows Class 02 No. 200 and its train leaving for Plymstock on 5th August 1928.

H. C. Casserley

A Class 02 No. 207 heads the Turnchapel train away from Lucas Terrace Halt on 22nd May 1935. A Class T9 is being turned on the turntable in the background.

H. C. Casserley

Two views looking east, of Plymstock's original LSWR station. Taken around 1910, they both show the line to Billacombe whilst only the lower shows the platform and line to Turnchapel and Oreston.

LGRP & Lens of Sutton

Oreston Station in LSWR days looking towards Plymstock.

Author

Oreston Station in BR days looking towards Plymstock.

W. E. Stevens

A photograph that epitomises the Turnchapel Branch. LSWR No. 218 crosses the swing bridge at Hooe Lake with its four-coach train on 8th July 1924.

H. C. Casserley

A Class 02, No. 233, with an Adams chimney, crosses Hooe Lake with its two-coach train on 14th June 1926.

H. C. Casserley

An early picture of a Class 02 and train at Turnchapel Station before auto working.

Lens of Sutton

Harry Caniford has an eye for the camera as Class 02, No. 218 and train reverses out of Turnchapel Station on the 8th July 1924.

H. C. Casserley

Plymstock Station, although busy, was not handling the 60 trains a day it claimed on the opening of the Yealmpton Branch at the turn of the century. Sadly however the Yealmpton Branch was closed to passenger traffic on 7th July 1930, an early casualty of the omnibus. Consequently there was of course less traffic over the Cattewater Junction to Plymstock section of the branch.

By 1935 further changes were afoot at Plymstock Station, a new signal box frame was opened in the booking office on 14th July of that year and the original was dismantled and the building demolished. In 1938 the closing of the refreshment rooms at Friary took place. They were later to become the new booking office following many rearrangements of the station building to suit new demands of the new imminent World War Two.

The effect of World War Two on the line was considerable in terms of damage and destruction. Friary Station, situated as it was in the centre of the city, received much attention from enemy attacks. The five Plymouth blitzes on the nights of 21st and 22nd March and 22nd, 23rd and 24th April 1941 caused Friary much superficial damage but strangely enough it survived the war structurally intact.

Not so the signal box and station buildings at Plymstock however, which were set alight by incendiary bombs during the 1941 blitzes and burnt out. Temporary 'replacement buildings' were built including a new signal box frame which opened on 12th October 1941. (These buildings remained until their demolition upon branch closure in the early 1960s

The most notable and dramatic event of wartime bombing came when the original terminus at Turnchapel was completely destroyed following an air raid on 27th November 1940. Ironically the attack was not on the station, but the naval and RAF oil storage tanks on either side of it were the targets. An excellent account of that fateful night is given by Bernard Darwin in the Southern Railway publication *War on the Line* and it is with due acknowledgement that I quote from the vividly descriptive narrative.

'Some description of the battlefield is necessary to the understanding of it. Turnchapel is on a branch line from Plymouth Friary Station which crosses by a three span bridge an inlet of Cattewater, called Hooe Lake. There is only one platform, at the back of which is a high rocky bank. Behind this bank is a hollow in which are several Admiralty oil tanks. On the opposite side of the track is another bank a good deal lower, and beyond this is land occupied by the RAF. After passing through the station the line runs to a tunnel communicating with the Admiralty Depot.

On the night of November 27th a German plane dropped four bombs: two fell harmlessly in the lake, one on the bridge, and one on an oil tank behind the rocky bank. The bomb on the bridge damaged the parapet and the signal box, and buried the signalman under the ruins of a shelter, from which he was dug out unhurt. The oil tank burst instantly into flames. The fire raged all through the night, and a signalman and a porter seeing the

The blazing oil tanks at Turnchapel during November 1940, which later ruptured and whose burning contents destroyed Turnchapel Station. *B. Thornton*

Below: A rare German wartime aerial photograph of the scene, which appeared in their propaganda magazine *Signaal* (printed in Dutch and dated 2nd May 1941). The branch can be seen running into the smoke, bottom left-hand corner.
Courtesy A. Joanknecht

danger to the station saved all the records at considerable risk to themselves. Next day the heat was so great that the water from the hose pipes evaporated before it could reach the flames, and deadly fumes made the work of fire fighting exceedingly dangerous. And then on the night following, that of Friday the 29th, the other tanks joined in the fray. The oil in them boiled over, and one exploded, scattering burning oil in all directions. Three AFS men were killed, and the others saved themselves by jumping into the water.

The blazing oil poured in a torrent over the rocky bank and down on to the station, obliterating it on the instant. It was like a living and malign thing, a river of fire struggling and tossing to break its way out from between its banks. It flooded the track for a length of 150 yards; it ran on to the bridge in one direction, and as far as the tunnel in the other. It climbed and crossed the lower bank on the further side of the track and so invaded the RAF, but luckily did no harm there. Next it fell on to the road leading to the station, flooded that and flowed on into the other river — of water. The channel is here 100 feet wide, but the oil took that in its fiery stride and set alight to a timber yard on the far side. Some of the blazing timber was thrown into the water and the rest was moved and saved.

It was not till the night of Sunday, December 1st, that the fire was at last put out. The station buildings had vanished, lamp standards and automatic machines survived as cripples, furiously twisted by the flames; the rails of the track were bent into fantastic shapes and the signal box which had partially withstood the bomb was now utterly destroyed. Yet in under a fortnight there was a temporary signal box and a newly laid track and freight trains were running; by the 16th passenger service was again normal'.

The other most significant event affecting the wartime life of the Turnchapel Branch was the reintroduction of passenger services on the former Yealmpton Branch on 3rd November 1941. Owing to the heavy bombing which had commenced earlier in the year, many of the surviving inhabitants of Plymouth strove to evacuate the city at night to the surrounding countryside. As a result all branch lines in the area experienced a definite upturn in passenger traffic and it was this fact that prompted the GWR to act. By now the railways were effectively 'nationalised' by their common war effort with many connections being made between adjacent companies' metals. The original terminus in Plymouth from which Yealmpton trains ran from 1898 to 1930 was of course Millbay.

Passenger traffic had ceased at Millbay on 23rd April 1941 following heavy damage, and was not to be restored. Mutley Station was closed to passengers on 3rd July 1939 in the interests of rationalisation by the GWR. Therefore the Yealmpton Branch now required another city terminus from which to run. Friary was the obvious choice and for six years between 1941 and 1947 the GWR ran the service from here.

This had a dramatic effect upon the traffic over the Friary—Lucas Terrace—Plymstock section of the line to Turnchapel.

Finally the preparations for the 'D' day landings in France brought a further surge of freight traffic to the Admiralty Wharves at Turnchapel, but apart from that the war ended without further significant events taking place along the branch.

The post-war years were to bring an early demise to the Turnchapel Branch. The first blow to be felt was the reclosure of passenger services on the Yealmpton Branch on 7th October 1947 following an announcement in the local press by the 'Southern & Great Western Joint Companies'. In retrospect, the closure was a little premature as the winter of 1947/8 turned out to be the worst in living memory and the retention of the Yealmpton train services for another six months might have prevented the western part of the South Hams from isolation.

On 4th April 1947 the *South Devon Times* reported that inhabitants of Turnchapel were considering raising a petition against the cancellation of the 10.45 p.m. train to Turnchapel and the 11.15 p.m. train to Plymouth, Friary. These trains did not feature on any printed time table as they were a wartime service. Southern Railway officials claimed acts of rowdyism and drunkenness were common on these trains and in fact they were patronised only because, at that hour, there were no buses available. The cancellation was implemented.

History of the Turnchapel Branch as part of British Railways until closure

On 1st January 1948 the branch became part of the new British Railways, Southern Region on the nationalisation of the railways. By now the 'writing was on the wall' for the closure of the line. Bus services from the city were expanding and becoming more frequent with 'Plymouth Joint Services' having been formed since 1st October 1942. Oil was comparatively cheap whereas coal on the other hand was becoming rapidly more expensive following the strikes for more pay by the country's coal miners. In fact, severe coal shortages during the winter of 1950/1 prompted the temporary closure of the branch from 14th January 1951. Regular passengers transferred their allegiance to the buses and although the service was restored on 2nd July 1951, much custom had been lost for ever.

Closure to passengers followed from 10th September 1951. The following weekend the *South Devon Times* carried a heading and 18 column inches recording the fact. There were the usual references to the hardship of longstanding passengers, the protestations from local inhabitants and councillors who hitherto had been indifferent to the fact that they had a railway into Plymouth. Aboard the last train were more passengers than had been seen for years, including members of the

Four views of 'The Devon Rambler', the only diesel multiple unit to traverse the branch and certainly the only passenger train to enter the Admiralty Wharves at Turnchapel. An R.E.C. special, it ran on the 11th April 1959 and is pictured at a) Plymstock Station; b) Oreston Station; c) crossing Hooe Lake on the return journey; d) Turnchapel Wharves.

C. Fennamore & R. E. Taylor

Two views of the R.C.T.S. special to Turnchapel on 2nd May 1959 as part of the Royal Albert Bridge celebrations: a) at Plymstock Station, b) at Turnchapel Station.

C. Fennamore & L. Crosier

Three views of the Plymouth Railway Circle 'last run' over the branch on 30th September 1961: a) at Plymstock Station, b) at Oreston Station, c) crossing the swing bridge over Hooe Lake.

L. Crosier & I. Hocking

Plymouth Railway Circle and boys from the Swarthmore Boys' Club. The latter aided by many casual passengers displayed the usual merriment and pageantry afforded to the death of a railway line at that time.

With the termination of regular public passenger services the inevitable specials were to be run from time to time. The first of these on Saturday 9th May 1953 was of unusual origin. Nicknamed 'The Titfield Thunderbolt', a one-coach train ran non-stop to Turnchapel from Friary carrying fifty members of the Plymouth Locospotters Club. The trip was organised by the then Odeon cinema to publicise their showing of the famous film of the same name that week.

It was not until Saturday 11th April 1959 that the next special, 'The Devon Rambler' appeared on the branch. It was the one and only time that a 3-car diesel multiple unit crossed the Plym and travelled to both Turnchapel and Yealmpton. It was organised by the Railway Enthusiasts' Club of Farnborough and the tour covered many branch lines in South Devon before returning home that evening to Farnborough.

Shortly afterwards, on Saturday 2nd May 1959, another special arrived. This time SR Class O2 No. 30182 with two familiar LSWR 'gate-type' coaches toured the line from Friary to Turnchapel and back, stopping at all stations. This special was organised by the Railway Travel & Correspondence Society as part of their Royal Albert Bridge centenary celebrations. GWR 0-6-0PT No. 6420 and two sets of auto coaches travelled to Yealmpton, but passengers transferred at Plymstock Station to SR Class O2 No. 30182 and train.

Just prior to the complete closure of the Yealmpton Branch on 29th February 1960, the Plymouth Railway Circle employing GWR 2-6-2T No. 4549 and nine brake vans ran a third special. Local newspaper accounts of the time claimed the train also covered the Turnchapel Branch although it is doubtful that the same locomotive power was used on this line. However be that as it may, it would have traversed the Friary to Plymstock section of the line in any case.

Finally in 1961 with the impending closure of the Turnchapel Branch to all traffic, the Plymouth Railway Circle organised yet another tour of the line employing SR Class M7 No. 30034 and eight brake vans. This special was run on Saturday 30th September 1961, just one month before the complete closure. Meanwhile Friary Station had itself closed to passengers on 15th September 1958, with Friary Junction Signal Box closing on 27th September the following year.

As time moved on into the autumn of 1961 the rundown and closures accelerated. Commencing on 2nd October Oreston Station closed to goods traffic with an extension until 20th October for timber from Bayly's, and Turnchapel Signal Box was also closed on 2nd October. The last full load of goods from Bayly's in fact left on 17th October and the final goods train left on 20th October as prescribed. A special CM&EE Department train with the recovered 'chairing machine' departed from Bayly's on 26th October 1961.

64

Last full goods train from Bayly's on 17th October 1961 crosses the bridge over Billacombe Road on its approach to Plymstock Station.

W. E. Stevens

BR diesel No. 11228 crosses Billacombe Road bridge with a C. M. & E. Dept train carrying the chairing machine from Bayly's on 26th October 1961.

W. E. Stevens

Track lifting at Stamps Bridge during March 1963.

Author

Demolition of Stamps Bridge on Sunday 12th May 1963.

Western Evening Herald

The deep cutting excavated to facilitate the new half-mile siding into the Associated Portland Cement Company works, north of Plymstock Station. 22nd June 1963.

Western Evening Herald

Demolition of the swing bridge across Hooe Lake on 28th October 1963.

Western Evening Herald

The final stages of demolition of the railway embankment between Billacombe Road and Stamps Bridges, south of Plymstock Station. (Former Station Master's house is in the top right of the picture). 8th April 1964.

Western Evening Herald

New road improvements and roundabout construction on the site of the old railway embankment south of Plymstock Station during August 1964.

Western Evening Herald

Plymstock Station, looking east during March 1963.

Author

A view of Turnchapel Station site in 1964 following the removal of the track and bridge.

Author

Following the complete closure of the railway beyond Plymstock, the newly completed road bridge over the River Plym, replacing the 'Iron Bridge', was opened, on 1st June 1962, by Lord Chesham, Parliamentary Secretary to the Minister of Transport. Friary 'B' Signal Box, the nearest to Friary Station, closed on 31st July 1962.

The years 1963—64 saw considerable demolition and redevelopment of the line. Track lifting commenced early in 1963 and had reached Stamps Bridge near to Plymstock Station by 14th March. Friary Motive Power Depot, together with Plymstock Signal Box, closed from 1st May and excavation work started within the confines of Plymstock Station about this time also. Stamps and Billacombe Road bridges were demolished during the early hours of two Sunday mornings on the 12th and 19th May 1963, respectively.

Redevelopment of the Friary to Plymstock section of the line

The *South Devon Times* for 21st January 1963 reported the fact that Plymstock Station was proving an exception to the wholesale closures of railways in the country, with a new half-mile extension of the line being blasted through 70,000 cubic yards of rock into the Associated Portland Cement Co. works at Saltram. By June that year the track was laid into the factory site by the Contractor, T. W. Ward Ltd., the Sheffield firm who were better known for much of the demolition of West Country railway lines following the 'Beeching Plan' at that time. The work when completed resulted in track running around the north side of the works and the construction of special loading platforms. British Rails had produced special cement carriers each with a capacity for 20 tons of bulk cement and one of the regular routes for the bulk loads was to be Chasewater in Cornwall where the company has a storage silo. Incoming freight traffic to the factory consists of quantities of paint and kiln bricks. The works at Plymstock were first opened in 1961, and the 1963 extension of the railway into the works cost the comany some £2 million.

The unique swing bridge across Hooe Lake to Turnchapel was dismantled and taken by road for scrap during October 1963. Early in March 1964 work commenced on the removal of the embankment between Billacombe Road and Stamps Bridge, which was completed by 8th April. A new roundabout and road-widening scheme was immediately started on the site of the old embankment and its construction was completed by early autumn.

During 1964—65 part of the site at Plymstock Station was being negotiated for by the South Western Gas Board for the construction of a depot to unload liquid petroleum gas. Work commenced during 1965 on the site, simultaneously with the building of the main gas production plant at Breakwater Works which started production of commercial gas the following year. Approximately 300 tons of liquid petroleum gas were

Three studies of BR diesel No. 4158 working trains at Plymstock on Wednesday 12th December 1973. a) Arriving at 11.45am with twelve liquid petroleum gas wagons, the second load that day; b) shunting cement wagons to clear space in the sidings; c) departing at 12.30 pm with the empty liquid petroleum gas wagons brought in full at 8.15am that day.

Author

arriving at Plymstock every week, to be piped on a 4 in. main under the adjoining roads to a giant 860 ton 'Horton Sphere' container at the works. The liquified gas Butane is carried in special rail containers at a 20 lb/sq. in. pressure and is used for enriching the lean gas produced at the works by increasing its calorific value by some 175 British Thermal Units. The final product then leaves the works by means of a high-pressure grid system of pipes.

In September 1965 Cattewater Junction Signal Box was dismantled and removed, with Friary 'B' Signal Box sharing the same fate the following month. The year 1965 saw great changes taking place at Friary Station itself. It was during October that year that the old goods station there was demolished and the BR freight handling complex construction commenced. This was duly completed and opened on 20th June 1966. Meanwhile all pointwork was disconnected from Friary 'A' Signal Box on 6th March 1966, the box closed on 24th April, and its removal executed later in 1966. During August of that year revised trackwork to serve the new goods complex was laid at Friary, completing the reorganisation of the site excepting for the passenger station. These decaying buildings were still in use in connection with freight and parcels traffic but mostly platform usage was apparent.

Finally, the late 1960s and early 1970s saw the trackbed below Radford Crossing disappear under the extension of Bayly Bartlett's timber yards; the Turnchapel Station site was levelled and taken into the confines of the now British Gas Corporation's oil storage depots; the trackbed between Stamps corner via Oreston Station to Radford Crossing became a public footpath and additional tracks were laid at Friary.

The final act to record with this short history must be the total demolition of Plymouth Friary Station during the period from March to May 1976. The grandiose dream of the London & South Western Railway had come to an end after 85 years. In 1981, only the Friary to Plymstock section remains as a siding to the cement works and liquid petroleum gas depot near to the site of the old station.

THE CATTEWATER BRANCH —
A Short History

The concept of this branch was closely intertwined with a complicated growth of a number of goods lines proposed by both the GWR and LSWR companies in the late 1870s.

By the mid 1870s both these companies had realised that Sutton Pool and the Cattewater presented a source of some considerable industrial revenue. The Plymouth & Dartmoor Co. as an ally of the LSWR proposed a number of extension railways based upon their Cattewater Branch concept. There were no less than five in total, covering ground ranging from Embankment Road to the Passage House Inn and Deadman's Bay. They were authorised by the 1875 Act of Parliament and the LSWR assumed powers over them under a further Act of 1882.

The actual Cattewater Branch opened sometime between 1879 and 1880 and the extension to the present terminus during 1888, although the actual dates are not recorded. Records of dates of both opening and closing of a goods line through a concentrated industrial development are very rare. The changing requirements of commercial trading results in continual changes in the companies participating during the life of the line (85 years in this case), and most are not recorded in any detail. However, to gain an insight into the subject, readers are invited to refer to the working instructions and sidings lists in the Chapter — **Engineering & Operating Data**. These are dated 1934 under Southern Railway operation and 1960 under British Railways operation.

Many sidings have been removed since 1960, two recorded are the Corporation Siding in November 1967 and the Regent Oil Siding in August 1969.

Perhaps the largest contributors to freight traffic in the earlier days on the branch were the former Plymouth 'A' Power Station, built in 1898 to supply the new trams with electricity, and the fertiliser firms. These were Charles Lorrington, Gibbs Fertilisers and Berard (Lack) & Algar, which all became part of the giant Fisons Group in post-war days and survived until recently. Plymouth 'A' Power Station was closed down in 1974 and demolished during 1975—6, causing the loss of much coal traffic to the branch.

The new power station, Plymouth 'B' was opened in 1952 with part of it still coal fired but this was later converted to oil burning during 1958—9. Although coal supplies to it may have been supplemented by rail, the main supplies of both coal and oil to the station were brought in by sea. Sadly, this power station too was phased out during 1981 and it ceased to supply the National Grid on 31st March that year. The 'mothballing' of the machinery was completed by August 1981.

It was also early in 1981 that the large Fisons fertiliser works closed with the loss of 120 jobs. Only a skeleton staff remained dismantling equipment, losing the branch a vast amount of freight traffic.

One would therefore presume that sidings serving the concern will soon be lifted and the Cattewater Branch will lose the major part of its current traffic. Oil from the Conoco and Esso depots with some liquid petroleum gas and Bitumen trains will provide the bulk of the remaining traffic in the near future. One may only speculate regarding the longer term future, on the survival of the branch into the 1990s.

New industry will undoubtedly arrive as the present recession ends and times improve, but the unfortunate trend in the past shows that new industry tends to employ road transport whilst BR strive to close a struggling line completely.

A recent aerial view of the Turnchapel area showing:– A) Admiralty Wharves with their truncated lines; B) the tunnel under Boringdon Road; C) the track-bed of the line from Turnchapel Station, the site of which is off picture at 'E'; D) the remains of Turnchapel steamer pier.

Western Morning News Ltd.

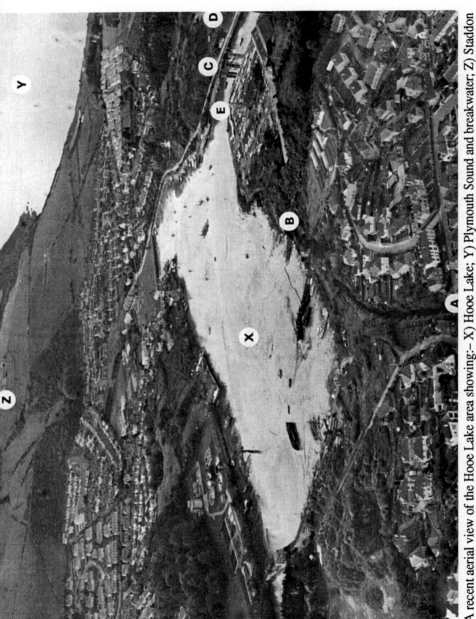

A recent aerial view of the Hooe Lake area showing:- X) Hooe Lake; Y) Plymouth Sound and breakwater; Z) Staddon Heights. Remains of the Turnchapel Railway are:- A)Bridge No. 6, carrying Plymstock Road; B)Radford Crossing; C) Piers of the Swing Bridge; D) Turnchapel Station site; E) Extended timber yards of Bayly Bartlett Ltd. c1980.

Western Morning News Ltd.

TIME TABLES AND BRANCH WORKING

Locomotives and stock employed on the branches

The locomotives can be categorised into two main classes from the opening of the line until the end of passenger working in 1951. These were the ex-LSWR Class 02 for all passenger working and the diminutive Class B4 for goods working.

Exceptions to this were the introduction, during the period 1904–1914 for summertime working, by the LSWR of Drummond Steam motor cars; Stock List Nos. 1 & 2; Carriage List Nos. 4201 & 4202. (They were transferred from the Basingstoke to Alton Railway for this task). Nos. 3–11 of order H13 are also believed to have had a turn on the branch.

A Class C14, 2–2–0T, made a rare appearance sometime during the period 1906–1917 before it was loaned to the Ministry of Munitions in April 1917 for some three years.

During the period 1930–1933, the ex-LBSC Class D1, No. 259 was used for push and pull working, whilst the 02s were so modified.

Class 02s recorded working the branch were:-
SR Nos. 177, 182, 207, 218, 225 & 233. (No. 218 was later to become W33 *Bembridge* on the Isle of Wight Railway in 1936).

BR Nos. 30182, 30183, 30207, 30216 & 30236.

Class B4s recorded working both branches were :-
SR Nos. 84, 91 & 102.

BR Nos. 30084, 30088, 30089, 30094 & 30102.

A picture of a very rare appearance of a LSWR class C14, 2–2–0T loco with auto trailers at Turnchapel Station. This loco, No. 741, one of ten of its class, derived from a Drummond steam motor car and, in February 1922, was converted to an 0–4–0T to improve rail adhesion, prior to being taken into SR stock and re-numbered 3741 during the 1923 amalgamation.

Lens of Sutton

In addition, during latter days of the Turnchapel branch, Class M7s were used for miscellaneous tasks. Those recorded were 30034, 30035, 30037 & 30040.

Diesel locomotives recorded for goods workings were:-
204 h.p. shunters Nos. DS 11227, 11228, 11234 & 11235.
0–6–0 No. D2128.

Specials

11th April 1959	– Railway Enthusiasts' Club of Farnborough
	Diesel Multiple Unit W51062 'Devon Rambler'
2nd May 1959	– Railway Travel & Correspondence Society
	Royal Albert Bridge Centenary
	Class 02 No. 30182
30th September 1961	– Plymouth Railway Circle
	Last trip on the branch
	Class M7 No. 30034
18th June 1966	– Plymouth Railway Circle
	Plymouth Suburban Railtour visiting Plymstock Station
	Class 03 No. D2178
21st December 1985	– Hertfordshire Rail Tours
	Last passenger train over Laira Bridge ('Gunnislake Goliath')
	Hastings '6L' DEMU

Coaching and rolling stock

LSWR 'Gate-Type' suburban stock Nos. S738 & S2622 = (S369 Set).
S734 & S3200.
GWR Special wagons for sleeper traffic Nos. 40420, 40421, 40411 & 40432 (Full load 120 sleepers each).

1970/1980 Goods traffic – Locomotives recorded:-
0–6–0 Diesel shunter No. 4158 for Plymstock cement and LPG traffic
0–6–0 Class 08 No. 08 659 for diesel oil, bitumen and Butane/Propane gas traffic on the Cattewater Branch.

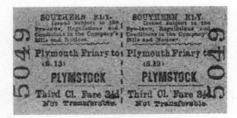

"Ticket peculiarity"? A S.R. "double single"
at 3^1/2d each and NOT a return!

N.B. Pages 82 & 83 are reproduced by kind permission of British Railways Board and, irrespective of the date, remains its exclusive copyright.

Class B4 No. 102 *Granville* in SR livery at Friary Motive Power Depot on 23rd June 1949.

S. C. Nash

The same locomotive, now appearing as No. 30102 in BR livery with its '1F' classification c1950s.

Author

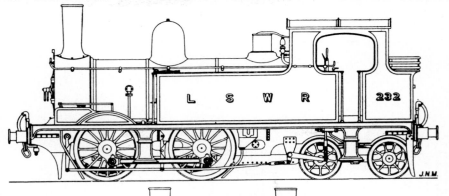

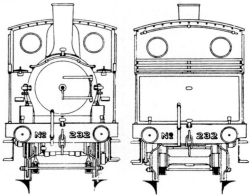

L.S.W.R. Class "O2" 0-4-4T No 232

A rare photograph of a Class D1, No. 259 at Turnchapel, working the branch during the early 1930s.

LGRP

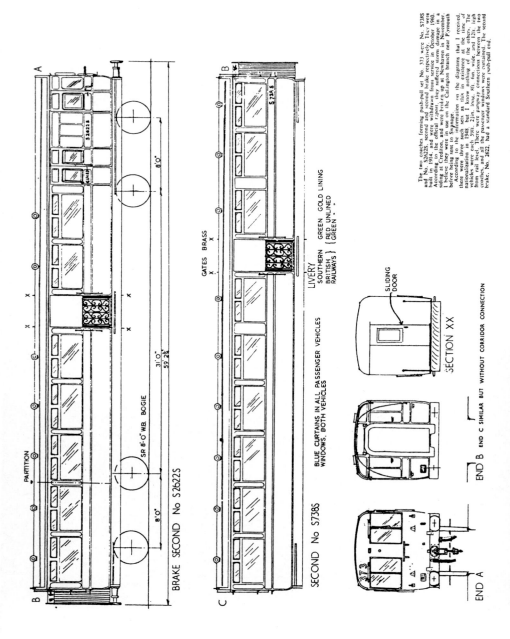

A

S26221S
6M119

PARTITION

SR 8'-0" W.B. BOGIE

8'-0"

31'-0"

59'-2½"

8'-0"

B

BRAKE SECOND No S2622S

B

S729-S

GATES   BRASS
x   x
x   x

LIVERY
SOUTHERN   GREEN GOLD LINING
BRITISH   } {RED UNLINED
RAILWAYS   } {GREEN * -"

C

SECOND No S738S

BLUE CURTAINS IN ALL PASSENGER VEHICLES
WINDOWS, BOTH VEHICLES

SLIDING
DOOR

SECTION XX

END B   END C SIMILAR BUT WITHOUT CORRIDOR CONNECTION

2733

END A

The two coaches forming push-pull set No. 373 were No. S738S and No. S2622S, second and second brake respectively. They were built in 1914, and were withdrawn from service in October 1960. According to the official report, they suffered storm damage in a siding at Crediton, and were broken up at Newhaven in November. I believe they were in use on the Callington branch near Plymouth before being sent to Swanage.

According to the information on the diagrams that I received, there were three such sets as this in existence at the time of nationalization in 1948 but I know nothing of the others. The vehicles were each 59ft. 2¼in. long, 8ft. 6in. wide, and 12ft. high from rail level. There were gangway connections between the two coaches, and all the passenger windows were curtained. The second brake, No. 2622, had a standard Southern push-pull end.

80

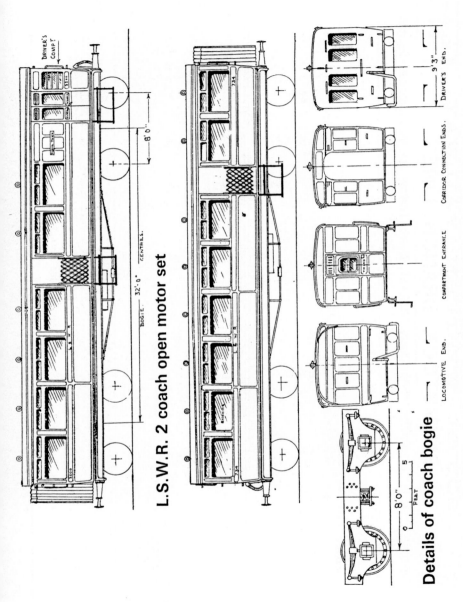

L.S.W.R. 2 coach open motor set

Details of coach bogie

By courtesy of the Railway Modeller. (Note, these carriage sets were used on this branch before their despatch to Callington Branch).

81

SOUTH WESTERN RAILWAY.
PLYMSTOCK BRANCH LINE.

INSTRUCTION No. 340, 1896.

Instructions as to the working of the Train Staff and Tickets between the undermentioned Sections, from January 1st, 1897, until further notice.

WEEK DAYS.—FRIARY TO PLYMSTOCK.

DOWN TRAINS.	1	2	3	4	5	6	7	8	9	10	11	12	13	14
	A Goods Staff.	A Goods Staff.	Staff.	B Goods Staff.	Staff.	Staff.	Staff.	Goods Staff.	Staff.	Staff.	Goods Staff.	Staff.	Staff.	A Goods Staff.
FRIARY ... ...dep.	a.m. 7 15	a.m. 8 15	a.m. 8 45	a.m. 9 25	a.m. 9 45	...	p.m. 1 40	p.m. 2 20	...	p.m. 3 30	p.m. 4 5	p.m. 5 25	p.m. 6 25	p.m. 7 0
CATTEWATER JUNC. ,,	...	...	...	9 28	...	...	...	...	...	...	4 9	...	...	7 4
CATTEWATER ... arr.	...	...	...	9 35	...	...	...	...	...	...	4 12	...	...	7 10
PLYMSTOCK ... ,,	7 20	8 20	8 50	...	9 50	...	1 45	2 25	...	3 35	...	5 30	6 30	...

WEEK DAYS.—PLYMSTOCK TO FRIARY.

UP TRAINS.	1	2	3	4	5	6	7	8	9	10	11	12	13	14
	A Goods Staff.	A Goods Staff.	Staff.	Staff.	B Goods Staff.	Staff.	Staff.	Staff.	Goods Staff.	Staff.	Staff.	Staff.	Staff.	A Goods Staff.
PLYMSTOCK ... ...dep.	a.m. 8 20	a.m. 8 30	a.m. 9 11	a.m. 10 36	p.m. 12 20	...	p.m. 2 0	...	p.m. 3 15	p.m. 3 51	p.m. 5 10	p.m. 5 45	p.m. 6 40	p.m. ...
CATTEWATER ... ,,	...	...	...	...	12 27	...	...	...	...	...	5 15	...	...	7 30
CATTEWATER JUNC. arr.	...	...	...	...	12 32	...	...	...	...	...	...	...	...	7 35
FRIARY ... ... ,,	8 25	8 35	9 16	10 41	...	...	2 5	...	3 20	3 55	5 20	5 49	6 45	7 40

A.—These Trains only run when required, and as ordered by Mr. Avery. When No. 1 Train runs, No. 2 will not run, and when No. 2 Train runs, No. 1 will not run.

B.—Mr. Avery, Friary, must send a man with this Train, who will, after the Train has been admitted to the Cattewater Branch and the points put in their normal position and locked by means of the Train Staff so that the Train cannot come out from the Cattewater Sidings until the Train Staff is again in the possession of the Driver, return with the Staff to the A Signal Box, Friary. The Signalman, on seeing the Train Staff, will electrically clear the road by Error Signal to Plymstock, in the usual way for Cattewater Trains, as if the Train had returned, after which the man will convey the Staff to Friary Station and hand it to Inspector Worth or Foreman in charge for the despatch of the 9.45 a.m. Down Train. On arrival of the 10.36 a.m. Train from Plymstock at Friary with the Train Staff, Mr. Avery will send the Staff in charge of the man to A Signal Box. The Signalman, on seeing the Staff in possession of the man, will, after seeing the Waving Signal to Plymstock and having obtained an acknowledgment, instruct him to proceed to the Cattewater Junction Points with the Staff to release the 12.20 p.m. Goods, and on the departure of the man with the Staff from A Signal Box the Signalman must send the Departure Signal to Plymstock in the same way as he would a Train, keeping the Line obstructed in the usual way until the 12.20 p.m. Goods from Cattewater arrives with the Train Staff, when the Line will be cleared in the usual way for Trains from Cattewater by Error Signal.

No Sunday Trains on this Branch.

WATERLOO BRIDGE STATION,
December, 1896.

(350)

BY ORDER.

(SEE OTHER SIDE.)

FRIARY, CATTEWATER, PLYMSTOCK AND TURNCHAPEL BRANCHES.—WEEK DAYS, JAN 1897

DOWN TRAINS.

Miles from Friary	DOWN TRAINS.	1 Goods. A	2 Goods. A	3 Pass.	4 Goods. B	5 Pass.	6	7 Pass.	8 Goods.	9 Goods. C	10 Pass.	11 Goods.	12 Pass.	13 Pass.	14 Goods. A
		arr. dep. a.m.	arr. dep. a.m.	arr. dep. a.m.	arr. dep. a.m.	arr. dep. a.m.		arr. dep. p.m.	arr. dep. p.m.	arr. dep. p.m.	arr. dep. p.m.	arr. dep. p.m.	arr. dep. p.m.	arr. dep. p.m.	arr. dep. p.m.
	FRIARY	... 7 15	8 20	... 8 45	... 9 25	... 9 45		... 1 40	... 2 20	...	... 3 30	...	... 5 25	... 6 25	7 0 7 4
	Cattewater Junction								2 25			4 8 4 9			7 7
	CATTEWATER		8 35									4 12			
	PLYMSTOCK	7 20 7 30		8 50 8 53	9 25 9 26	9 50 9 53		1 45 1 48		2 30 2 33	3 35 3 38	4 5	5 30 5 33	6 30 6 33	7 10
	Oreston	7 33			9 35					2 35					
	Bayly's Siding														
	TURNCHAPEL	7 35		8 55		9 55		1 50			3 40		5 35	6 45	
	" (WHARF)	7 37													

NO SUNDAY TRAINS.

UP TRAINS.

Miles from Turnchapel	UP TRAINS.	1 Goods. A	2 Goods. A	3 Pass.	4 Pass.	5 Goods. B	6	7 Pass.	8 Goods. C	9 Goods.	10 Pass.	11 Goods.	12 Pass.	13 Pass.	14 Goods. A
		arr. dep. a.m.	arr. dep. a.m.	arr. dep. a.m.	arr. dep. a.m.	arr. dep.		arr. dep. p.m.	arr. dep. p.m.	arr. dep. p.m.	arr. dep. p.m.	arr. dep. p.m.	arr. dep. p.m.	arr. dep. p.m.	arr. dep. p.m.
	TURNCHAPEL (Wharf)	... 8 5													
	Turnchapel	8 10		9 5	10 30			1 54			3 45		5 35		
	Bayly's Siding												5 39		
	Oreston	8 13		9 8	10 33			1 57			3 48		5 42		
	PLYMSTOCK	8 15 8 20		9 11	10 36	12 20		2 0	3 0		3 51	5 10	5 45	6 40	7 30
	CATTEWATER		8 30						3 2	3 15		5 13 5 15			7 34
	Cattewater Junction					12 27			3 5			5 20			7 35
	FRIARY	8 25	8 35	9 16	10 41	12 32		2 5		3 20	3 55		5 49	6 45	7 40

NO SUNDAY TRAINS.

This is a Single Line and is worked under the Train Staff and Ticket System as well as under the absolute Block Telegraph System, as between Friary, Cattewater Junction and Plymstock, and under Tyers' (New) Train Tablet System, as between Plymstock and Turnchapel.

A These Trains will run only as required and as ordered by Mr. Avery. When No. 1 Train runs No. 2 will not run, and when No. 2 Train runs No. 1 will not run. The load of Goods Trains on the Cattewater Branch must not exceed 30 loaded wagons and 1 van.

B Mr. A. Avery, Friary, must send a man with this Train, who will, after the Train has been admitted to the Cattewater Branch and the points put in their normal position and locked by means of the Train Staff, that is, that the Train cannot come out from the Cattewater Sidings until the Train Staff is again in the possession of the Driver, return with the Staff to the A Signal Box, Friary, the Signalman, on seeing the Train Staff, will electrically clear the road by Error Signal to Plymstock, in the usual way for Cattewater Trains, as if the Train had returned, after which the man will convey the Staff to Friary Station and hand it to Inspector Worth or Foreman in charge for the despatch of the 9.45 a.m. Train to Turnchapel. On arrival of the 10.30 a.m. Train from Turnchapel at Friary with the Train Staff, Mr. Avery will send the Staff in charge of the man to A Signal Box, the Signalman, on seeing the Staff in possession of the man, will, after sending the Warning Signal to Plymstock and having obtained an acknowledgment, instruct him to proceed to the Cattewater Junction Points with the Staff to release the 12.20 p.m. Goods, and on the departure of the man with the Staff from A Signal Box the Signalman must send the Departure Signal to Plymstock in the same way as he would for a Train keeping the Line obstructed in the usual way until the 12.20 p.m. Goods from Cattewater arrives with the Train Staff, when the Line will be cleared in the usual way for Trains from Cattewater by Error Signal.

C These Trains will run only as required, and as ordered by the Station Master at Plymstock.

The above supersedes that shown on page 163 of the Main Line Service Book for October and 119 for November.

FRIARY, CATTEWATER, PLYMSTOCK AND TURNCHAPEL BRANCHES.

FOR SPEED RESTRICTIONS SEE PAGES A, B, C & D.

This is a Single Line as between Friary "A" Box and Turnchapel, between which points is worked under the Regulations for working Single Lines by the Electric Train Tablet System.

The L. & S. W. Co.'s Passenger Service between Plymouth, Plymstock and Turnchapel is worked by means of a Steam Motor Car, 1st and 3rd Class only. The G. W. Co.'s Passenger Service between Plymouth and Yealmpton is worked by Steam Motor Car, one Class only.

WEEK DAYS.

WEEK DAYS—continued.

SUNDAYS.

FRIARY, CATTEWATER, PLYMSTOCK AND TURNCHAPEL BRANCHES.

FOR SPEED RESTRICTIONS SEE PAGES A, B, C & D.

This is a Single Line as between Friary "A" Box and Turnchapel, between which Points it is worked under the Regulations for working Single Lines by the Electric Train Tablet Block System.

The L. & S. W. Co.'s Passenger Service between Plymouth, Plymstock and Turnchapel is worked by Steam Motor, 1st and 3rd Class only. The G. W. Co.'s Passenger Service between Plymouth and Yealmpton is worked by Steam Motor Car, one Class only.

WEEK DAYS.

WEEK DAYS—continued.

SUNDAYS.

PLYMOUTH (FRIARY) AND TURNCHAPEL.
(THIRD CLASS ONLY.)

WEEK DAYS ONLY.

		a.m.	a.m.	a.m.	a.m.	a.m.	a.m.	a.m.	a.m.	a.m.	p.m.	p.m.	p.m.	p.m.	p.m.	p.m.	p.m.	p.m.	p.m.	p.m.	p.m.	p.m.	p.m.	
Plymouth (Friary)	dep	5 45	6 22	7 30	8 19	9 10	9 55	10 5	9 5	1 33	12	2 5	1 32	2 5	2 55	3 27	3 53	4 22	5 35	5 50	6 42	7 20	8 27	
Lucas Terrace Halt	,,	5 47	6 24	7 32	8 21	9 11	10 1	11	11	1 33	12 5	7	1 33	3 7	2 57	3 29	3 55	4 24	5 15	5 52	6 44	7 26	8 29	
Plymstock	,,	5 51	6 29	7 36	8 25	2 25	10 11	11	3 11	3 12	12 12	12 5	1 36	3 11	3 0	3 2	3 58	4 27	5 19	5 56	6 47	7 30	8 33	
Oreston	,,	5 53	6 31	7 38	8 37	9 28	10 13		11 4	12 1	13 50	1 4	2 18		3 31	1	4 30	4 30	5 21	5 54	6 50	7 32	8 35	
Turnchapel	arr	5 55	6 33	7 40	8 29	9 20	10 15		1 43	2 15	1	1 43	2 15		3 33		4 32	5 23	6 0	6 52	7 3	8 37		

WEEK DAYS ONLY CONTINUED

		p.m.	p.m.																					
Plymouth (Friary)	dep	9 7	10 2	11 10																				
Lucas Terrace Halt	,,	9 9	10 4	11 12																				
Plymstock	,,	9 13	10 8	11 16																				
Oreston	,,	9 15	10 10	11 18																				
Turnchapel	arr	9 17	10 12	11 20																				

WEEK DAYS ONLY.

		a.m.	a.m.	a.m.	a.m.	a.m.	a.m.	a.m.			p.m.	p.m.	p.m.		p.m.	p.m.	p.m.	p.m.	p.m.	p.m.	p.m.	p.m.	p.m.	
Turnchapel	dep	6 0	6 35	8 0	9 32	9 3	10 19		1	2 31	1 5	1 4	2 19		3 39	4 7	4 34	5 30	6 22	6 55	7 57	8 42	
Oreston	,,	6 3	6 3	8 2	9 34	10 22	10 21		11 5	12 3	1	1 4	2 21		3 41	5 0	4 36	5 32	6 24	7	7 59	8 44	
Plymstock	,,	6 6	6 36	8 6	9 37	9 36	10 24	11 10	11 8	12 6	1 10	1 8	2 24	3 14	3 44	4 13	4 40	5 36	6 27	7	9	8 48	
Lucas Terrace Halt	,,	6 8	6 44	8 8	9 40	9 3	10 2	11 14	11 6	12 9	1 1	1 54	2 27	3 17	3 47	4 15	4 42	5 38	6 39	7	6	8 50	
Plymouth (Friary)	arr	6 10	6 45	8 10	8 42	9 40	10 29	11 15	11 6	1 1	1 55	2 29	3 19	3 49	4 17	4 44	5 40	6 39	7	8 4	7 8	8 52	

WEEK DAY ONLY CONTINUED.

		p.m.	p.m.	p.m.																				
Turnchapel	dep	9 18	10 15	11 22																				
Oreston	,,	9 21	10 17	11 24																				
Plymstock	,,	9 24	10 20	11 27																				
Lucas Terrace Halt	,,	9 27	10 23	11 30																				
Plymouth (Friary)	arr	9 29	10 25	11 32																				

A Wednesdays, Fridays and Saturdays only.

Public Passenger Time Table for June to September 1914.

FRIARY TO PLYMSTOCK AND TURNCHAPEL. SOUTHERN RAILWAY.

Fares from Friary. To Lucas Terrace Halt, third single 1½d. To Plymstock, third single 2¼d., To Oreston, third single 3d., third return 5½d. To Turnchapel, third single 3d., third return 5½d.

Week Days only. Third Class only.

		A M		A M		A M		A M		A M		A M	A M	A M	P M		P M		P M		P M		P M
Friary	d.	5 43	...	6 20	...	7 20	...	8 17	...	8 50	...	9 53	11 27	12 12	...	12 48	...	1 25	...	2 8	...	3 23
Lucas Terrace Halt	..	5 47	...	6 22	...	7 22	...	8 19	...	8 52	...	9 55	11 29	12 14	...	12 50	...	1 27	...	2 5	...	3 25
Plymstock	..	5 51	...	6 26	...	7 26	...	8 33	...	8 55	...	9 59	11 33	12 18	...	12 54	...	1 31	...	2 9	...	3 29
Oreston	..	5 53	...	6 28	...	7 28	...	8 25	...	8 58	...	10 1	11 35	12 20	...	12 56	...	1 33	...	2 11	...	3 51
Turnchapel	a.	5 55	...	6 30	...	7 30	...	8 37	...	9 0	...	10 3	11 37	12 22	...	12 58	...	1 35	...	2 13	...	3 53

		P M		P M	P M	P M		P M		P M		P M	P M	P M	P M								
Friary	d.	4 19	...	4 53	5 22	5 53	...	6 36	...	7 30	...	8 20	9 0	9 55	10 50								
Lucas Terrace Halt	..	4 21	...	4 55	5 24	5 55	...	6 38	...	7 32	...	8 22	9 2	9 57	10 52		No Sunday service						
Plymstock	..	4 25	...	4 59	5 28	5 59	...	6 42	...	7 36	...	8 26	9 6	10 1	10 56								
Oreston	..	4 27	...	5 1	5 30	6 1	...	6 44	...	7 38	...	8 28	9 8	10 3	10 59								
Turnchapel	a.	4 29	...	5 3	5 32	6 3	...	6 46	...	7 40	...	8 30	9 10	10 5	11 3								

		A M		A M		A M		A M		A M		A M	A M	A M	P M		P M		P M		P M		P M
Turnchapel	d.	6 0	...	6 35	...	7 50	...	8 32	...	9 3	...	10 7	11 42	12 28	...	1 3	...	1 39	...	2 21	...	3 37
Oreston	..	6 2	...	6 37	...	7 52	...	8 34	...	9 5	...	10 9	11 44	12 30	...	1 5	...	1 41	...	2 23	...	3 19
Plymstock	..	6 5	...	6 40	...	7 55	...	8 37	...	9 8	...	10 12	11 47	12 33	...	1 8	...	1 44	...	2 26	...	3 42
Lucas Terrace Halt	..	6 8	...	6 43	...	7 58	...	8 40	...	9 11	...	10 15	11 50	12 36	...	1 11	...	1 47	...	2 29	...	3 45
Friary	a.	6 10	...	6 45	...	8 0	...	8 42	...	9 13	...	10 17	11 52	12 38	...	1 13	...	1 49	...	2 31	...	3 47

		P M	P M	P M		P M	P M		P M	P M	P M		P M	P M	P M								
Turnchapel	d.	4 33	5 35	5 37	...	6 15	7	...	8 28	8 40	...	9 22	...	10 15	11 8								
Oreston	..	4 35	5 7	5 39	...	6 17	7 9	...	8 48	8 42	...	9 24	...	10 17	11 10		No Sunday service						
Plymstock	..	4 38	5 10	5 42	...	6 20	7 12	...	8 7	8 45	...	9 27	...	10 20	11 13								
Lucas Terrace Halt	..	4 41	5 13	5 45	...	6 23	7 15	...	8 10	8 48	...	9 30	...	10 23	11 16								
Friary	a.	4 43	5 15	5 47	...	6 25	7 17	...	8 12	8 50	...	9 32	...	10 25	11 20								

Public Passenger Time Table for January 1925 & U.F.N. Published by W. Brendon & Son Ltd.

FRIARY, CATTEWATER, PLYMSTOCK AND TURNCHAPEL BRANCHES.

The Passenger Service between Friary, Plymstock and Turnchapel is worked by an Engine and Cars (3rd Class only).

Distances		M. C.	M. C.	M. C.	M. C.	M. C.	M. C.	M. C.	M. C.
		0 65	0 75	2 19	1 44	2 00	2 26	2 46	3 55

WEEK-DAYS DOWN TRAINS		Friary.	Lucas Ter. Halt.	Cattewater Jct.	Catte-water.	Plym-stock.	Oreston.	Bayley's Siding.	Turn-chapel.	Turnchapel Wharf.
		dep.	dep.	Pass	arr.	dep.	arr.	arr.	arr.
a.m. S.R.	Pass. C	6 35	6 39	5 40¼	...	5 43	5 45	...	5 47
,, ,, ,,		6 20	6 22	6 23½	...	6 26	6 28	...	6 30

...

SUNDAYS, 17th JULY to 25th SEPTEMBER only.

B—Arrives 11.26 p.m.   C—Arrives 5.37 a.m.

SR (Western Division) Working Time Table of Passenger and Freight Trains from 17th July 1932 & U.F.N.

86

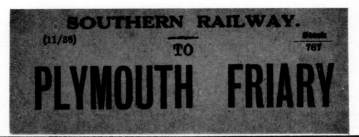

SOUTHERN RAILWAY.
(11/36)
TO
PLYMOUTH FRIARY
Book 787

PLYMOUTH (FRIARY), PLYMSTOCK AND TURNCHAPEL BRANCH.

The Passenger Service between Plymouth Friary, Plymstock and Turnchapel is worked by an Engine and Cars (3rd Class only).

Distances		M. C.	M. C. 0 55	M. C. 0 75	M. C. 1 44	M. C. 2 00	M. C. 2 45	Distances		M. C. 0 0	M. C. 0 45	M. C. 1 01	M. C. 1 50	M. C. 1 70	M. C. 2 45
WEEKDAYS. DOWN TRAINS.		Friary.	Lucas Ter. Halt.	Catte-water Jet.	Plym-stock.	Oreston.	Turn-chapel.	WEEK-DAYS. UP TRAINS.		Turn-chapel.	Oreston.	Plym-stock.	Catte-water Jct.	Lucas Ter. Halt.	Friary.
		dep.	dep.	pass	dep.	dep.	arr.			dep.	dep.	dep.	pass	dep.	arr.
a.m.	S.R.	5 35	5 39	5 40½	5 43	5 45	5 47	a.m.	S.R.	5 55	5 57	6 0	6 1½	6 3	6 5
"	"	6 18	6 20	6 21½	6 24	6 26	6 28	"	"	6 33	6 35	6 38	6 39½	6 41	6 43
"	G.W.	6 43	6 50	6 51½	6 54	6 56	6 58	"	"	7 3	7 5	7 8	7 9½	7 11	7 13
"	S.R.	7 0	7 2	7 3½	7 6			"	"	7 42	7 44	7 47	7 48½	7 50	7 52
"	"	7 28	7 30	7 31½	7 34	7 36	7 38	"	G.W.			8 2	8 3½	8 5	8 7
"	S.R.	8 17	8 19	8 20½	8 23	8 25	8 27	"	S.R.	8 29	8 31	8 34	8 35½	8 37	8 39
"	"	8 48	8 50	8 51½	8 54	8 56	8 58	"	"	9 3	9 5	9 8	9 9½	9 11	9 13
"	G.W.	8 53	8 55	8 56½	8 59			"	G.W.			9 50	9 51½	9 53	9 55
"	G.W.	10 33	10 35	10 35½	10 39			"	S.R.	11 3	11 5	11 8	11 9½	11 11	11 13
p.m.	S.R.	10 40	10 42	10 43½	10 46	10 48	10 50	"	G.W.			11 39	11 40½	11 42	11 44
"	"	12 15	12 17	12 18½	12 21	12 23	12 25	p.m.	S.R.	12 28	12 30	12 33	12 34½	12 36	12 38
"	G.W.	12 48	12 50	12 51½	12 54	12 56	12 58	"	"	1 3	1 5	1 8	1 9½	1 11	1 13
"	S.R.	1 14	1 16	1 17½	1 20			"	"	1 39	1 41	1 44	1 45½	1 47	1 49
"	"	1 26	1 28	1 29½	1 32	1 34	1 36	"	G.W.			2 1½	2 18½	2 20	2 22
"	"	2 5	2 7	2 8½	2 11	2 13	2 15	"	S.R.	2 20	2 22	2 25	2 26½	2 28	2 30
"	G.W.	2 50	2 52	2 53½	2 56			"	"			3 52	3 53½	3 55	3 57
"	S.R.	4 22	4 24	4 25½	4 28	4 30	4 32	"	"	4 35	4 37	4 40	4 41½	4 43	4 45
"	G.W.	4 57	4 59	5 0½	5 3	5 5	5 7	"	"	5 9	5 11	5 14	5 15½	5 17	5 19
"	S.R.	5 20	5 22	5 23½	5 26			"	G.W.	5 52	5 54	5 57	5 58½	6 0	6 2
"	"	5 39	5 41	5 42½	5 45	5 47	5 49	"	"			6 17	6 18½	6 20	6 22½
"	"	5 30	6 32	6 33½	5 36	6 38	6 40	"	G.W.	6 45	6 47	6 50	6 51½	6 53	6 55
"	G.W.	6 40	6 42	6 43½	6 46			"	S.R.			7 37	7 38½	7 40	7 42
"	S.R.	7 30	7 32	7 33½	7 36	7 38	7 40	"	"	7 50	7 52	7 55	7 56½	7 58	8 0
"	"	8 30	8 32	8 33½	8 36	8 38	8 40	"	"	8 50	8 52	8 55	8 56½	8 58	9 0
"	"	9 9	9 11	9 12½	9 15	9 17	9 19	"	"	9 22	9 24	9 27	9 28½	9 30	9 32
"	G.W.	9 45	9 47	9 48½	9 51			"	"	10 30	10 32	10 35	10 36½	10 38	10 40
"	S.R. SO	10 15	10 17	10 18½	10 21	10 23	10 25	"	G.W. SO			10 55	10 56½	10 58	11 0

A—To Yealmpton, G.W.R.   O—From Yealmpton, G.W.R.

PLYMOUTH (FRIARY), CATTEWATER, PLYMSTOCK AND TURNCHAPEL BRANCHES.

Distances		M. C. 0 00	M. C. 0 75	M. C. 2 19	M. C. 1 44	M. C. 2 00	M. C. 2 26	M. C. 2 45	Distances		M. C. 0 00	M. C. 0 19	M. C. 0 45	M. C. 1 01	M. C. 1 50	M. C. 2 45
WEEK-DAYS. DOWN TRAINS.		Friary.	Cattewater Jct.	Catte-water.	Plym-stock.	Oreston.	Bayly's Siding.	Turn-chapel.	WEEK-DAYS. UP TRAINS.		Turn-chapel.	Bayly's Siding.	Oreston.	Plym-stock.	Catte-water Jct.	Friary.
		dep.	Pass	arr.	dep.	dep.	arr.	arr.			dep.	dep.	dep.	dep.	dep.	arr.
a.m.	S.R.	7 22	7 25	7 28	7 28				a.m.	S.R.			10 20			10 26
"	"	9 15	9 18		9A21				"	S.R. EQ	11 50		11 53	12C0 O		12 9
"	" Q	11 15	11 18		11C21		11 29		"	"			12 3		12 9	12 12
"	" Q	11 15	11 18		11C21		11 29		p.m.	S.R.		11 55		12C0 3		
"	G.W.			11 33		11 36		To Yealmpton.	"	" Q				12 55	12 58	1 1
						11 50			"	G.W.				2 58		3 0
p.m.	S.R.	11 55	11 58	12					"	" Q				4 35		4 37
"	" SX	2 32	2 35		2C38		2 46		"	S.R. Q	4 42	4 45	4 56			5 5 5 11
"	" SX	2 45	2 48	2 51					"	"		4 53	5 4			
"	" Q	4 0	4 3		4 6			4 14	"	"				5 50	5 52	5 56
"	" Q	5 10	5 13	5 16					"	"				6 54	6 56	7 1
"	" Q	6 26	6 29	6 35					"	" SX				8 40	8 43	8 46

A—Arrival time.   C—Passing time.   D—Will not run when 11.15 a.m. to Bayly's Siding runs.   E—Will not run when 11.55 a.m. from Bayly's Siding runs.

SR (Western Division, Section E) Working Time Tables of Passenger and Freight Trains from 16th June 1947 & U.F.N.

PLYMOUTH and TURNCHAPEL (3rd class only)

Week Days

	mrn mrn mrn mrn mrn mrn mrn	aft aft aft aft aft aft aft	aft aft aft	aft aft
Plymouth (Friary)..dep.	5 35 6 18 6 48 7 28 8 16 8 48 1040 ..	1215 1245 1 21 2 5 4 22 4 57 5 52 ..	6 30 7 30 8 30 ..	9 9 1015
Lucas Terrace Halt..	5 37 6 19 6 49 7 29 8 17 8 49 1041 ..	1216 1246 1 22 2 6 4 23 4 58 5 49 ..	6 31 7 31 8 31 ..	9 19 1016
Plymstock..........	5 42 6 23 6 53 7 33 8 21 8 53 1045 ..	1220 1250 1 28 2 10 4 27 5 2 5 44 ..	6 35 7 35 8 35 ..	9 14 1020
Oreston............	5 44 6 25 6 55 7 35 8 23 8 55 1047 ..	1222 1253 1 32 2 14 4 29 5 4 5 44 ..	6 37 7 37 8 37 ..	9 16 1022
Turnchapel........arr.	5 47 6 28 6 58 7 38 8 26 8 58 1050 ..	1225 1256 1 34 2 19 4 32 5 7 5 49 ..	6 40 7 40 8 40 ..	9 19 1025

Week Days

	mrn mrn mrn mrn mrn mrn mrn	aft aft aft aft aft aft	aft aft aft aft aft
Turnchapel.......dep.	5 56 6 33 7 37 43 .. 8 29 9 3 11 3 ..	1231 1 39 2 20 4 35 5 9 ..	5 52 6 45 7 59 8 50 9 22 1030
Oreston............	5 56 6 34 7 47 43 .. 8 30 9 4 11 4 ..	1229 1 41 40 2 21 4 36 5 10 ..	5 53 6 46 7 51 8 51 9 23 1031
Plymstock.........	5 59 6 37 7 77 46 .. 8 33 9 7 11 7 ..	1231 1 71 43 2 24 4 39 5 13 ..	5 56 6 49 7 54 8 54 9 26 1034
Lucas Terrace Halt ..	6 2 6 49 7 10 7 49 .. 8 36 9 10 11 10 ..	1235 1 10 1 46 2 27 4 42 5 16 ..	5 59 6 52 7 57 8 57 9 29 1 37
Plymouth (Frry) 3 45 arr.	6 5 6 43 7 13 7 52 .. 8 39 9 13 11 13 ..	1238 1 13 1 49 2 30 4 45 5 18 ..	6 2 6 55 4 9 0 9 32 1049

Sundays

Plymouth (Friary)..dep.	..	..	..	..	..	..	..	..	..	..
Lucas Terrace Halt	..	..	..	..	..	..	..	..	..	..
Plymstock.............	..	..	..	..	..	..	..	..	..	..
Oreston..............	..	..	..	..	..	..	..	..	..	..
Turnchapel.......arr.	..	..	..	..	..	..	..	..	..	..

Sundays

Turnchapel ....dep.	..	..	..	..	..	..	..
Oreston	..	..	..	..	..	..	..
Plymstock	..	..	..	..	..	..	..
Lucas Terrace Halt	..	..	..	..	..	..	..
Plymouth (Frry) 345 arr.	..	..	..	..	..	..	..

S R Passenger Time Table for 5th May 1941 U.F.N.

Table 66		PLYMOUTH, PLYMSTOCK, and TURNCHAPEL

Ⓢ—All Trains are Third class only

Week Days only

	a.m a.m a.m a.m	a.m a.m a.m a.m	p.m p.m p.m p.m p.m p.m p.m p.m p.m p.m p.m p.m p.m p.m
Plymouth (Friary)..dep	5 35 5 15 4 45 7 25	8 17 8 45 1046	1216 1245 1 26 2 5 4 04 22 5 7 25 2 5 20 7 20 5 10 6 30 1030
Lucas Terrace Halt	5 37 5 19 4 49 7 29	8 18 8 49 1047	1217 1244 1 2 2 6 1 5 2 5 1 40 6 31 7 31 5 31 9 31 1031
Plymstock............	5 42 5 23 6 53 7 33	8 20 8 53 1045	12 0 1250 1 31 2 10 3 54 27 5 12 5 44 6 35 7 35 5 35 9 35 1035
Oreston	5 44 5 25 6 55 7 36	8 24 8 55 1047	1220 1250 1 33 2 12 3 .. 7 4 29 5 14 5 46 6 37 7 37 5 37 9 37 1037
Turnchapel ....arr	5 47 5 28 6 57 7 38	8 27 8 58 1050	12 5 1255 1 30 2 15 3 10 4 32 5 17 5 49 6 40 7 40 4 40 4 40 1040

Week Days only

	a.m a.m a.m a.m	a.m a.m a.m a.m	p.m p.m p.m p.m p.m p.m p.m p.m p.m p.m p.m p.m p.m
Turnchapel ....dep	5 55 6 33 7 42	4 29 3 11 3	1231 1 39 2 20 4 18 4 35 5 10 5 72 6 47 7 50 8 45 1045
Oreston	5 56 6 34 7 47 43	3 30 4 11 4	1239 1 41 40 2 21 4 16 4 36 5 20 5 56 6 46 7 51 8 46 46 1046
Plymstock...........	5 59 6 37 7 46	3 33 7 11 7	1231 1 45 1 24 3 19 4 39 5 23 5 56 6 49 7 54 8 49 49 1049
Lucas Terrace Halt	6 2 6 47 10 7 49	3 36 10 11 10	1235 1 10 1 40 2 27 3 22 4 45 5 26 5 59 6 52 7 57 8 52 1052
Plymouth (Friary) ..arr	6 8 6 43 7 13 7 52	3 39 0 11 13	1236 1 13 1 49 2 30 3 25 4 48 5 29 1 6 55 8 0 8 59 53 1055

541

BR (SR) Last Passenger Time Table, for 18th June to 23rd September 1951.

Table 1 (Down — morning)

Mileage M	C		№	am	am	Q am	am	From Baylys Siding am	W.R. to Yealmpton MW FO am	L E am	(Not when 10.10 am E.B.V Plymouth Friary runs)	From Laira Q am	From Laira Q noon			
0	0	P'MOUTH FRIARY ⊤dep	1	6 28	8 5	9 0	9 15	..	am	10∥45	..	..	12 0	..	..	..
0	75	Cattewater Jn. ⊤	2	6 31	8 8	9 3	9 18	..	10 45	10 48	..	10 55	12 3	..	..	..
2	19	CATTEWATER arr	3	6 34	8 11	9 6	..	..	..	10∥51	..	10 58	12 6	..	..	..
1	44	Plymstock ⊤ arr	4				9 21	10 18		10 48		..	..			
		⊤ dep	5				9 36	10 32		10 58		..	..			
2	0	Oreston dep	6									..	..			
2	26	Baylys Sidings arr	7				9 44					..	..			
2	45	TURNCHAPEL ⊤ arr	8						10 40			..	..			

Table 2 (Down — afternoon)

Station	№	L E SX PM	SX PM	PM	From Baylys Siding SX PM	E.B.V from Laira SX PM	SX PM	Q PM					
PLYMOUTH FRIARY dep	1	2 15	2 32	2∥55	..	4 0	..	6 35	..	..	..	..	..
Cattewater Jn.	2	2 18	2 35	2 58	..	4 3	5 5	6 38	..	..	..	..	..
CATTEWATER arr	3	2 21	..	3∥1	..	4 6	5 8	6 41	..	..	..	..	..
Plymstock arr	4		2 38		3 23								
dep	5		2 50		3 27								
Oreston	6												
Baylys Sidings arr	7		2 58										
TURNCHAPEL arr	8				3 35								

Table 3 (Up — morning)

Mileage M	C		№	To Turnchapel Q am	am	am	am	W.R. from Yealmpton MW FO PM	Q PM	To Turnchapel SX PM					
0	0	TURNCHAPEL ⊤dep	1	..	..	..	11 15	..	..	..	..	..	..	..	..
0	19	Baylys Siding dep	2	..	10 10	..	..	..	..	3 15	..	..	..	..	..
0	45	Oreston arr	3	..			11 18				..	..	..	..	..
		dep	4				11 28				..	..	..	..	..
1	1	Plymstock ⊤arr	5		10 18		11 31			3 23	..	..	..	..	..
		⊤dep	6		10 32		11 41	1 13		3 27	..	..	..	..	..
0	0	CATTEWATER dep	7	10 30		11 15			1 30		..	..	..	..	..
1	50	Cattewater Jn. ⊤	8	10 33	10 33	11 18	11 44	12 58	1 33		..	..	..	..	..
2	45	P'MOUTH FRIARY ⊤arr	9	10 36		11 21	11 47	1 1	1 36		..	..	..	..	..

Table 4 (Up — afternoon)

Station	№	W.R. from Yealmpton SX Q PM	To Laira Q PM	SX PM	SX PM	PM	SX PM	SX PM	SX Q PM				
TURNCHAPEL dep	1	..	..	..	4 42	..	..	..	..	..	..	..	..
Baylys Siding dep	2									..	..	..	..
Oreston arr	3				4 45					..	..	..	..
dep	4				4 53					..	..	..	..
Plymstock arr	5				4 56					..	..	..	..
dep	6		3 35		5 0					..	..	..	..
CATTEWATER dep	7	3 30	..	4 30	..	5 30	6 5	7 45	8 45	..	..	..	..
Cattewater Jn.	8	3 33	3 37	4 33	5 3	5 33	6 8	7 48	8 48	..	..	..	..
PLYMOUTH FRIARY arr	9	3 36	..		5 6	5 36	6 11	7 51	8 51	..	..	..	..

BR Southern Operating Area (Western Division) Section K, Working Time Tables of Freight Trains from 11th June 1956 & U.F.N.

Daily	SuX	SuX	SuX	SuX	SuX	SuX					WSO
	am	am	am	am	am	am	am			pm	pm
Plymouth (Princess Sq.)	6 30	7 5	7 35	8 5	8 35	9 5	9 35			1035	11 5
Oreston	6 43	7 18	7 48	8 18	8 48	9 18	9 48			1048	1118
Hooe *	6 55	7 30	8 0	8 30	9 0	9 30	10 0	Then		11 0	1130

	SuX	SuX	SuX	SuX	SuX	SuX		every 30			WSO
	am	am	am	am	am	am	am	mins.		pm	pm
Hooe *	6 55	7 36	8 6	8 36	9 6	9 36	10 6	until		11 6	1136
Oreston	7 7	7 48	8 18	8 48	9 18	9 48	1018			1118	1148
Plymouth (Princess Sq.)	7 20	8 1	8 31	9 1	9 31	10 1	1031			1131	12 1

* - ¼ mile to Turnchapel Station.
SuX - Sundays excepted.   WSO - Wednesdays and Saturdays only.

15 minute frequency (except Sunday mornings) between Plymouth and Oreston, these additional buses operating to and from Goosewell Cross.

ORESTON AND TURNCHAPEL FERRY TIMETABLE   August 1950

Daily		SuX	SuX	SuX						SuO	SO	SSuX	SuO	SO
		am	am	am	am	am	am	am	am	am	am	am	am	am
Plymouth	dep.	7B30	8B 5	8 35	9 0	9 35	10 0	1035	11 0	1120	1130	1135	1140	1155
Turnchapel	"	7 40	8 15	8 45	9 10	9 45	1010	1045	1110	1130	1140	1145	1150	12 5
Oreston	arr.	....	....	....	9 15	....	1015	....	....	....	....	....	....	....

		SX	SO	SX	SO							SSuX	SSuO	SSuX
		noon	pm	pm	pm	pm	pm	pm	pm	pm	pm	pm	pm	pm
Plymouth	dep.	12 0	1220	1235	1240	1 0	1 35	2 0	2 35	3 0	3 35	4 0	4 0	4 30
Turnchapel	"	1210	1 30	1245	1250	1 10	1 45	2 10	2 45	3 10	3 45	4 10	4 10	4 40
Oreston	arr.	1215	....	....	....	1 15	....	2 15	....	3 15	....	....	4 15	....

		SSuO	SSuX	SSuO	SSuX	SSuO	SSuX							
		pm	pm	pm	pm	pm	pm	pm	pm	pm	pm	pm	pm	pm
Plymouth	dep.	4 35	4 55	5 0	5 20	5 35	5 40	6 0	6 35	7 0	7 35	8 0	8 35	9 0
Turnchapel	"	4 45	5 5	5 10	5 30	5 45	5 50	6 10	6 45	7 10	7 45	8 10	8 45	9 10
Oreston	arr.	....	....	5 15	....	....	....	6 15	....	7 15	....	8 15	....	9 15

		pm	pm					SuX	SuX	SuX				
Plymouth	dep.	9 35	10 0		Oreston	dep.	am	am	am	am	am	am	am	am
Turnchapel	"	9 45	1010		Turnchapel	"	....	....	....	....	9 15	....	1015	
Oreston	arr.	....	....		Plymouth	arr.	7 20	7 50	8 25	8 50	9 25	9 50	1025	

Plymouth arr. 7 30 8 0 8 35 9 0 9 35 10 0 1035

		SuO	SO	SSuX	SuO	SO	SX	SO	SX	SO			
		am	am	am	am	am	am	pm	pm	pm	pm	pm	pm
Oreston	dep.	....	....	....	....	....	....	....	1215	....	....	1 15	....
Turnchapel	"	1050	1110	1120	1125	1130	1145	1150	1235	1225	1230	1250	1 25	1 50
Plymouth	arr.	11 0	1120	1130	1135	1140	1155	12 0	1215	1235	1240	1 0	1 35	2 0

						SSuX	SSuO	SSuX	SSuO	SSuX	SSuO	SSuX	
		pm	pm	pm	pm	pm	pm	pm	pm	pm	pm	pm	pm
Oreston	dep.	2 15	....	3 15	....	....	4 15	....	....	....	5 15	....	....	6 15
Turnchapel	"	2 25	2 50	3 25	3 50	4 20	4 25	4 45	4 50	5B 5	5 25	5 30	5 50	6 25
Plymouth	arr.	2 35	3 0	3 35	4 0	4 30	4 35	4 55	5 0	5 15	5 35	5 40	6 0	6 35

		pm	pm	pm	pm	pm	pm	pm
Oreston	dep.	....	7 15	....	8 15	....	9 15	....
Turnchapel	"	6 50	7 25	7 50	8 25	8 50	9 25	9 50
Plymouth	arr.	7 0	7 35	8 0	8 35	9 0	9 35	10 0

B - Calls at Mount Batten.   SuX - Sundays excepted.   SuO - Sundays only.
SO - Saturdays only.   SSuX - Saturdays and Sundays excepted.   SX - Saturdays excepted.
SSuO - Saturdays and Sundays only.

Oreston & Turnchapel Steamboat Co., Ltd., H.R. Elford, Managing Director, Oreston, Plymouth.

MOUNT BATTEN · HOOE LAKE · DEAN CROSS · ORESTON · ROYAL PARADE · PLYMOUTH RAILWAY STATION · DEVONPORT (6) · MOLESWORTH ROAD (7) · ST. BUDEAUX · BULL POINT · SALTASH PASSAGE

JULY 1965 U.F.N.

Weekdays

	6	6	6	6	7	6	Spl	6	6	6	7	7	6	7	6	7	6	7	6	7
MOUNT BATTEN (B'House)								0554					0725		0755	0810		0840	0855	
Mount Batten (G/Room)								0556				0657	0727		0757	0812		0842	0857	0927
Hooe Lake							P	0559		0615	0629	0644	0700	0715	0730	0745	0800	0815	0830	0845	0900	0915	0930	0945
Dean Cross					0557			0606		0622	0636	0651	0707	0722	0737	0752	0807	0822	0837	0852	0907	0922	0937	0952
Oreston					0600			0609		0625	0639	0654	0710	0725	0740	0755	0810	0825	0840	0855	0910	0925	0940	0955
Laira Bridge Road Garage	0458	0513	0540	0546	0601	0604	0606	0614	0618	0630	0644	0659	0715	0730	0745	0800	0815	0830	0845	0900	0915	0930	0945	1000
The Viaduct	0505	0520	0547	0553	0608	0611	0612	0621	0625	0637	0651	0706	0722	0737	0752	0807	0822	0837	0852	0907	0922	0937	0952	1007
Royal Parade	0506	0521	0548	0554	0609	0612	0613K	0622	0626	0638	0652	0707	0723	0738	0753	0808	0823	0838	0853	0908	0923	0938	0953	1008
Devonport	0520		0602	0608		0626	0625	0636		0652		0737		0807		0837		0907		0937		1007	
South Keyham Gate	0523			0611	0625		0628	0639		0655	0709	0724	0740	0755	0810	0825	0840	0855	0910	0925	0940	0955	1010	1025
H.M.S. Drake	0528			0616	0631		0633	0644		0700	0714	0729	0745	0800	0815	0830	0845	0900	0915	0930	0945	1000	1015	1030
St. Budeaux (Square)	0534			0622			0639	0650		0706	0720	0735	0751	0806	0821	0836	0851	0906	0921	0936	0951	1006	1021	1036
Bull Point								0655		0711	0725	0740	0756	0811	0826	0841	0856	0911	0926	0941	0956	1011	1026	1041
SALTASH PASSAGE				0628			0645	0700		0716	0730	0745	0801	0816	0831	0846	0901	0916	0931	0946	1001	1016	1031	1046

	6			7	6	7	8			6	7	6	7	6	7	6	7	6	7	6	7
MOUNT BATTEN (B'House)								1641	1656		1726				1826						
Mount Batten (G/Room)	0957		27	..	57			1612	1627	1643	1658		1728	1742	1757		1828		1855		1926		2006		2046		2126
Hooe Lake	1000		15	30	45	0		1615	1630	1646	1701	1715	1731	1745	1800	1815	1831	1847	1856	1907	1929	1947	2009	2027	2049	2107	2129
Dean Cross	1007		22	37	52	7		1622	1637	1653	1708	1722	1738	1752	1807	1822	1838	1854	1905	1914	1936	1954	2016	2034	2056	2114	2136
Oreston	1010		25	40	55	10		1625	1640	1656	1711	1725	1741	1755	1810	1825	1841	1857	1908	1917	1939	1957	2019	2037	2059	2117	2139
Laira Bridge Road Garage	1015		30	45	0	15		1630	1645	1701	1716	1730	1746	1800	1815	1830	1846	1902	1913	1922	1944	2002	2024	2042	2104	2122	2144
The Viaduct	1022		37	52	7	22		1637	1652	1708	1723	1737	1753	1807	1822	1837	1853	1909		1929	1951	2009	2031	2049	2111	2129	2151
Royal Parade	1023		38	53	8	23		1638	1653	1709	1724	1738	1754	1808	1823	1838	1854	1910		1930	1952	2010	2032	2050	2112	2130	2152
Devonport	1037			7	..	37			1707		1738		1808		1852		1944		2004		2044		2124	
South Keyham Gate	1040		55	10	25	40		1655	1710	1726	1741	1755	1811	1825	1840	1855		1927		1947	2009	2027	2049	2107	2129	2147	2209
H.M.S. Drake	1045		0	15	30	45		1700	1715	1731	1746	1800	1816	1830	1845	1900		1932		1952	2014	2032	2054	2112	2134	2152	2214
St. Budeaux (Square)	1051		6	21	36	51		1706	1721	1737	1752	1806	1822	1836	1851	1906		1938		1958	2020	2038	2100	2118	2140	2158	2220
Bull Point	1056		11	26	41	56		1711	1726	1742	1757	1811	1827	1841	1856	1911		1942			2024		2104		2144		2224
SALTASH PASSAGE	1101		16	31	46	1		1716	1731	1747	1802	1816	1832	1846		1916					2004		2044		2124		2204

(column: then at the following mins. past each hour until)

CODE
P—From Plymstock Church dep. 0550.
K—Operated via Union Street, King's Road and Devonport (Park Avenue).

Spl—Special Journey, subject to alteration or suspension at short notice subject to requirements of Government Establishments.

SALTASH PASSAGE · BULL POINT · ST. BUDEAUX · MOLESWORTH ROAD (7) · DEVONPORT (6) · PLYMOUTH RAILWAY STATION · ROYAL PARADE · ORESTON · DEAN CROSS · HOOE LAKE · MOUNT BATTEN

Weekdays

	Spl	6	6	6	7	6	7	6	6	6	6	7	6		6	7	6	7	6	7
SALTASH PASSAGE							0630	0647	0702	0718	0732	0747	0803	0818	0633	0848		3	18	33	48	1518	1533	1548
Bull Point							0635	0652	0707	0723	0737	0752	0808	0823	0638	0853		8	23	38	53	1523	1538	1553
St. Budeaux (Square)			0538				0640	0657	0712	0728	0742	0757	0813	0828	0643	0858		13	28	43	58	1528	1543	1558
H.M.S. Drake			0542				0633	0648	0703	0718	0734	0748	0803	0819	0834	0849	0904	19	34	49	4	1534	1549	1604
South Keyham Gate			0547				0638	0651	0708	0723	0739	0753	0806	0824	0839	0854	0909	then at 24	39	54	9	1539	1554	1609
Devonport				0550	0605		0608		0654		0726		0756		0827		0857	27	..	57	..		1557	
Royal Parade		0523		0603	0618	0628	0641	0654	0709	0724	0729	0755	0809	0824	0840	0855	0910	0925 following 40	55	10	25	1553	1610	1625
The Viaduct		0525		0605	0620	0630	0643	0656	0709	0726	0741	0757	0811	0826	0842	0857	0912	0927 minutes 42	57	12	27 until	1557	1612	1627
Laira Bridge Road Garage		0532	0532	0558	0612	0627	0637	0650	0703	0718	0733	0748	0804	0818	0833	0849	0904	0919 0934 each 49	4	19	34	1604	1619	1634
Dean Cross		0537	0537	0603	0617	0632	0642	0655	0708	0721	0738	0753	0809	0823	0838	0854	0909	0924 hour 54	9	24	39	1609	1624	1639
Oreston			0540	0540	0606	0620	0635	0645	0658	0711	0724	0741	0756	0812	0826	0841	0857	0912 0927 0942	57	12	27	42	1612	1627	1642
Hooe Lake		P	0547	0613	0627	0642	0652	0705	0718	0731	0748	0803	0819	0833	0848	0904	0919 0934 0949	4	19	34	49	1619	1634	1649
Mount Batten (G/Room)		0550			0655		0721		0751	0806		0836	0851		0922		0952	22	..	52		1622	1637	1652
MOUNT BATTEN (B'House)		0552			0723		0753	0808		0838	0853											1639	1654

	6	7	6	7	6	7	6	7	6	7	6	7	6	7	6	7	6	7
SALTASH PASSAGE	1603	1618	1633	1648	1703	1718	1733	1749	1804	1821	1844	1854		1924		2006		2046		2126		2208		2248		2334
Bull Point	1608	1823	1838	1853	1708	1723	1738	1754		1826		1906		1946		2026		2106		2146		2226		2306	
St. Budeaux (Square)	1613	1828	1543	1658	1713	1728	1743	1759	1810	1830	1850	1900	1910	1930	1950	2012	2030	2052	2110	2132	2150	2212	2230	2252	2310	2340
H.M.S. Drake	1619	1634	1649	1704	1719	1734	1749	1805	1818	1838	1858	1908	1918	1936	1956	2018	2036	2058	2116	2138	2156	2218	2236	2258	2316	2346
South Keyham Gate	1624	1639	1654	1709	1724	1739	1754	1810	1821	1841	1901	1911	1921	1941	2001	2023	2041	2103	2121	2143	2201	2223	2241	2303	2321	2351
Devonport	1627		1657		1727		1757		1824		1904	1914		1944		2026		2106		2146		2226		2306		2354
Royal Parade	1642	1657	1712	1727	1742	1757	1812	1828	1839	1859	1919	1929	1939	1959	2019	2041	2059	2121	2139	2201	2219	2241	2259	2321	2339	0009
The Viaduct	1644	1657	1712	1727	1742	1757	1812	1828	1839	1859	1919	1929	1939	1959	2019	2041	2059	2121	2139	2201	2219	2241	2259	2321	2339	0009
Laira Bridge Road Garage	1649	1704	1719	1734	1749	1804	1819	1835	1846	1906	1926	1936	1946	2006	2026	2048	2106	2128	2146	2208	2226	2248	2306	2328	2346	0016
Oreston	1654	1709	1724	1739	1754	1809	1824	1840	1851	1911	1931		1951	2011	2031	2053	2111	2133	2151	2213	2231	2253	2311	
Dean Cross	1657	1712	1727	1742	1757	1812	1827	1843	1854	1914	1934		1954	2014	2034	2056	2114	2136	2154	2216	2234	2256	2314	
Hooe Lake	1704	1719	1734	1749	1804	1819	1834	1850	1901	1941		2001	2021	2041	2103	2121	2143	2201	2223	2241	2303	2321	
Mount Batten (G/Room)	1722	1737	1752		1822		1853		1924		2004		2044		2124		2204	2228	2244		2324	
MOUNT BATTEN (B'House)	1724				1824										2228			2326	

CODE
P—To Plymstock Church arr. 0547.

Spl—Special journey, subject to alteration or suspension at short notice to requirements of Government Establishments.

MOUNT BATTEN · HOOE LAKE · DEAN CROSS · ORESTON · ROYAL PARADE · PLYMOUTH RAILWAY STATION · DEVONPORT (6) · MOLESWORTH ROAD (7) · ST. BUDEAUX · BULL POINT · SALTASH PASSAGE

JULY 1965 U.F.N.

Weekdays

	6	7	6	7	6	7
MOUNT BATTEN (B'House)	......	......	2230	......	......	2328
Mount Batten (G/Room)	......	2206	2232	2248	......	2330
Hooe Lake	2147	2209	2235	2248	2307	2333
Dean Cross	2154	2216	2242	2256	2314	2340
Oreston	2157	2219	2245	2259	2317	2343
Laira Bridge Road Garage	2202	2224	2250	2304	2322	2348
The Viaduct	2209	2231	2257	......	......	......
Royal Parade	2210	2232	2258	......	......	......
Devonport	2224	......	2312	......	......	......
South Keyham Gate	2227	2249	2315	......	......	......
H.M.S. Drake	2232	2254	2320	......	......	......
St. Budeaux (Square)	2238	2300	2326	......	......	......
Bull Point	......	2304	......	......	......	......
SALTASH PASSAGE	2244	......	2332	......	......	......

Sundays

	6	7	6	7	6	7	6	7	6	7	6	7	6	7	6	7	6
MOUNT BATTEN (B'House)																	
Mount Batten (G/Room)				0912		1012		1114		1214			1314		1352		
Hooe Lake			0645	0915	0945	1015	1045	1117	1145	1217		1245	1317	1338	1355	1415	
Dean Cross			0852	0922	0952	1022	1052	1124	1152	1224		1252	1324	1342	1402	1422	
Oreston			0855	0925	0955	1025	1055	1127	1155	1227		1255	1327	1345	1405	1425	
Laira Bridge Road Garage	0800	0630	0900	0930	1000	1030	1100	1132	1200	1232	1248	1300	1332	1350	1410	1430	
The Viaduct	0807	0637	0907	0937	1007	1037	1107	1139	1207	1239	1255	1307	1338	1357	1417	1437	
Royal Parade	0808	0638	0908	0938	1008	1038	1108	1140	1208	1240	1256	1308	1340	1358	1418	1438	
Devonport	0822	......	0922	......	1022	......	1122	......	1222	......	1310	1322	......	1412	......	1452	
South Keyham Gate	0825	0855	0925	0955	1025	1055	1125	1157	1225	1257	1313	1325	1357	1415	1435	1455	
H.M.S. Drake	0830	0900	0930	1000	1030	1100	1130	1202	1230	1302	1318	1330	1402	1420	1440	1500	
St. Budeaux (Square)	0836	0906	0936	1006	1036	1106	1136	1206	1236	1308	1324	1336	1408	1426	1446	1506	
Bull Point	......	0910	......	1010	......	1110	......	1212	......	1312	......	......	1412	......	1450	......	
SALTASH PASSAGE	0842	......	0942	......	1042	......	1142	......	1248	......	1330	1342	......	1436	......	1512	

	7		6	7	6	7	6	7
MOUNT BATTEN (B'House)								
Mount Batten (G/Room)	1434	then every 40 mins. until		2154		2234	2300	2314
Hooe Lake	1437			2157	2215	2237	2303	2317
Dean Cross	1444		2142	2204	2222	2244	2310	2324
Oreston	1447	then every 20 mins. until	2145	2207	2225	2247	2313	2327
Laira Bridge Road Garage	1452		2150	2212	2230	2252	2318	2332
The Viaduct	1459		2157	2219	2237	......	......	......
Royal Parade	1500		2158	2220	2238	......	......	......
Devonport	......	then every 40 mins. until	2212	......	......	......	......	......
South Keyham Gate	1517		2215	2237	......	......	......	......
H.M.S. Drake	1522	then every 20 mins. until	2220	2242	......	......	......	......
St. Budeaux (Square)	1528		2226	2248	......	......	......	......
Bull Point	1532	then every 40 mins. until	......	2252	......	......	......	......
SALTASH PASSAGE	......	then every 40 mins. until	2232	......	......	......	......	......

SALTASH PASSAGE · BULL POINT · ST. BUDEAUX · MOLESWORTH ROAD (7) · DEVONPORT (6) · PLYMOUTH RAILWAY STATION · ROYAL PARADE · ORESTON · DEAN CROSS · HOOE LAKE · MOUNT BATTEN

Sundays

	6	7	6	7	6	7	6	7	6	7	6	7	6	6	7	6			7	6	6
SALTASH PASSAGE	0640	......	0844	......	0944	......	1044	......	1144	......	1244	1332	1352	......	1434	then every 40 mins. until			......	2154	......
Bull Point	0645	......	......	0912	......	1014	......	1114	......	1214	......	......	1314	......	1414	then every 40 mins. until			2134	......	......
St. Budeaux (Square)	0650	......	0850	0916	0950	1018	1050	1118	1150	1218	......	1250	1318	1338	1358	1418	1440		2138	2200	
H.M.S. Drake	0656	......	0856	0922	0958	1024	1056	1124	1156	1224	......	1256	1324	1344	1404	1424	1446	then every 20 mins. until	2144	2206	
South Keyham Gate	0701	......	0901	0927	1001	1029	1101	1129	1201	1229	......	1301	1329	1349	1409	1429	1451		2148	2211	
Devonport	0704	......	0904	......	1004	......	1104	......	1204	......	......	1304	......	1352	1412	......	1454		......	2214	......
Royal Parade	0717	......	0917	0943	1017	1045	1117	1145	1217	1245	......	1317	1345	1405	1425	1445	1507		2205	2227	2242
Laira Bridge Road Garage	0726	0827	0851	0926	0952	1026	1054	1126	1154	1226	1254	1318	1326	1354	1414	1434	1454	1516	then every 20 mins. until	2207	2229	2243
Oreston	......	0832	0856	0931	0957	1031	1059	1131	1159	1231	1259	1323	1331	1359	1419	1439	1459	1521		2214	2236	2250
Dean Cross	......	0835	0859	0934	1000	1034	1102	1134	1202	1234	1302	1326	1334	1402	1422	1442	1502	1524		2219	2241	2255
Hooe Lake	......	0842	0906	0941	1007	1041	1109	1141	1209	1241	1309	1333	1341	1409	1429	1449	1509	1531		2222	2244	2258
Mount Batten (G/Room)	......	......	0909	......	1010	......	1112	......	1212	......	1312	......	1344	......	1432	......	1512	......	then every 40 mins. until	2229	2251	2305
MOUNT BATTEN (B'House)																				2232	2254	2308
																				......	2256	2310

	7	6	7
SALTASH PASSAGE	......	2234	......
Bull Point	2214	......	2254
St. Budeaux (Square)	2218	2240	2258
H.M.S. Drake	2224	2246	2304
South Keyham Gate	2229	2251	2309
Devonport	......	2254	......
Royal Parade	2245	2307	2325
The Viaduct	2247	2309	2327
Laira Bridge Road Garage	2254	2316	2334
Oreston	......	......	......
Dean Cross	......	......	......
Hooe Lake	......	......	......
Mount Batten (G/Room)	......	......	......
MOUNT BATTEN (B'House)	......	......	......

SALTASH PASSAGE - CITY CENTRE MOUNT BATTEN **September 1979 U.F.N.**

Via Wolseley Road, Rennie Avenue, Foulston Avenue, Poole Park Road, Wolseley Road, Saltash Road, Keyham Road, Park Avenue, Fore Street, Paradise Road, Wilton Street, Stuart Road, Plymouth Station, Western Approach, Union Street, Royal Parade, Exeter Street, Embankment Road, Laira Bridge, Pomphlett Road, Horn Cross Road, Stanborough Road, Dunstone Drive, Dolphin Court Road, Goosewell Road, Green Park Road, Hooe Road and Church Hill.

Weekdays

																		●	
SALTASH PASSAGE	......	......	0630	0650	0700	0720	0735	0750	Then	20	35	50	05 Mins		1720	1735	1750	1813	1828
St. Budeaux Square	0545	......	0640	0700	0710	0730	0745	0800	every	30	45	00	15 past		1730	1745	1800	1823	1838
Devonport (Granby Way)	0558	0633	0653	0713	0723	0743	0758	0813	15	43	58	13	28 each		1743	1758	1813	1836	1851
ROYAL PARADE (Stop L)	0614	0629	0649	0709	0729	0739	0759	0814	mins	59	14	29	44 hour		1759	1814	1829	1852	1907
Laira Bridge (W.N. Garage)	0622	0637	0657	0717	0737	0747	0807	0822	at	07	22	37	52 until		1807	1822	1837	1900	1915
Plymstock (Library)	0628	0643	0703	0723	0743	0753	0813	0828	0843	13	28	43	58		1813	1828	●	1906	......
Hooe Lake	0637	0652	0712	0732	0752	0802	0822	0837	0852	22	37	52	07		1822	1837	1852	1915	......
MOUNT BATTEN (RAF Recpt.)	0643	0658	0718	0738	0758	0808	0828	0843	0858	28	43	58	13		1828	1843	1858	1921	......

Sundays

SALTASH PASSAGE	1843		13	43	2243	2311	2341	0913	1013	1113	1143		13	43	2243	2311	2341
St. Budeaux Square	1853	Then	23	53	2253	2321	2351	0923	1023	1123	1153	Then	23	53	2253	2321	2351
Devonport (Granby Way)	1906	every	36	06 past	2306	2334	▲	0936	1036	1136	1206	every	36	06 past	2306	2334	▲
ROYAL PARADE (Stop L)	1922	30	52	22 each	2322	2350	......	0952	1052	1152	1222	30	52	22 each	2322	2350	......
Laira Bridge (W.N. Garage)	1930	mins	00	30 hour	2330	2358	0014	1000	1100	1200	1230	mins	00	30 hour	2330	2358	0014
Plymstock (Library)	1936	at	06	36 until	2336	......	......	1006	1106	1206	1236	at	06	36 until	2336	......	......
Hooe Lake	1945		15	45	2345	......	......	1015	1115	1215	1245		15	45	2345	......	......
MOUNT BATTEN (RAF Recpt.)	1951		21	51	2351	......	......	1021	1121	1221	1251		21	51	2351	......	......

Weekdays

MOUNT BATTEN (RAF Recpt.)	......	......	0539	......	0620	0635	0650		05	20	35	50		1650	1705	1723	1738	1758
Hooe Lake	......	......	0545	......	0626	0641	0556	Then	11	26	41	56 Mins		1656	1711	1729	1744	1804
Plymstock (Library)	......	......	0554	......	0635	0650	0705	every	20	35	50	05 past		1705	1720	1738	1753	1813
Laira Bridge (W.N. Garage)	0505	0542	0540	0600	0630	0641	0656	0711	15	26	41	56 11 each		1711	1726	1744	1759	1819
ROYAL PARADE (Stop L)	0513		0548	0608	0618	0638	0651	0706	0721	mins	36	51	06 21 hour		1721	1736	1754	1809	1829
Devonport (Granby Way)	0527	▲	0602	0622	0632	0652	0705	0720	0735	at	50	05	20 35 until		1735	1750	1808	......	1843
St. Budeaux Square	0540	0615	0615	0635	0645	0705	0718	0733	0748		03	18	33 48		1748	1803	1821	......	1856
SALTASH PASSAGE			0625	0645	0655	0715	0728	0743	0758		13	28	43 58		1758	1813	1831	......	1906

MOUNT BATTEN (RAF Recpt.)	1828		28	28	2228	2258	2326	0758	0858	0958	1028	1058		28	58	2228	2258	2326
Hooe Lake	1834	Then	04	34 Mins	2234	2304	2332	0804	0904	1004	1034	1104	Then	04	04 Mins	2234	2304	2332
Plymstock (Library)	1843	every	13	43 past	2243	2313	2341	0813	0913	1013	1043	1113	every	13	43 past	2243	2313	2341
Laira Bridge (W.N. Garage)	1849	30	19	49 each	2249	2319	2347	0819	0919	1019	1049	1119	30	19	49 each	2249	2319	2347
ROYAL PARADE (Stop D)	1859	mins	29	59 hour	2259	2327	......	0829	0929	1029	1059	1129	mins	29	59 hour	2259	2327	......
Devonport (Granby Way)	1913	at	43	13 until	2313	......	......	0843	0943	1043	1113	1143	at	43	13 until	2313	......	......
St. Budeaux Square	1926		56	26	2326	......	......	0856	0956	1056	1126	1156		26	56	2326	......	......
SALTASH PASSAGE	1936		06	36	2336	......	......	0906	1006	1106	1136	1206		36	06	2336	......	......

Additional Depot Journeys: Mount Batten to Laira Bridge Garage, direct via Radford Park Road at 1803 NSu, 1833 NSu, 1903 NSu, 2366.
Laira Bridge to Mount Batten direct via Radford Park Road. Weekdays dep. 0516, 0557, 0612, 0657, Sundays 0735, 0835, 0935, 1035, 1135

CODE: ▲ Direct via Cobourg Street and Milehouse
● Service 7A via Oreston (1842) and Drakes Drum (1844)

SALTASH PASSAGE - CITY CENTRE - CATTEDOWN - MOUNT BATTEN **October 1980 U.F.N.** 7

Via Wolseley Road, Rennie Avenue, Foulston Avenue, Poole Park Road, Wolseley Road, Saltash Road, Keyham Road, Park Avenue, Fore Street, Paradise Road, Wilton Street, Stuart Road, Plymouth Station, Western Approach, Union Street, Royal Parade, Exeter Street, Sutton Road, Commercial Road, Alvington Street, Elliott Road, Heles Terrace, Embankment Road, Laira Bridge, Pomphlett Road, Horn Cross Road, Stanborough Road, Dunstone Drive, Dolphin Court Road, Goosewell Road, Green Park Road, Hooe Road and Church Hill.

Sundays

Saltash Passage	0920	1000	1040	1120	1200	1240	1320	1400	1440	1520	1600	1640	1720	1800	1840	1920	2000	2040	2120	2200
St. Budeaux Square	0930	1010	1050	1130	1210	1250	1330	1410	1450	1530	1610	1650	1730	1810	1850	1930	2010	2050	2130	2210
Devonport (Granby Way)	0943	1023	1103	1143	1223	1303	1343	1423	1503	1543	1623	1703	1743	1823	1903	1943	2023	2103	2143	2223
Royal Parade	0959	1039	1119	1159	1239	1319	1359	1439	1519	1559	1639	1710	1759	1839	1919	1959	2039	2119	2159	2239
Laira Bridge (W.N. Garage)	1013	1053	1133	1213	1253	1333	1413	1453	1533	1613	1653	1733	1813	1853	1933	2013	2053	2133	2213	2253
Plymstock (Library)	1019	1059	1139	1219	1259	1339	1419	1459	1539	1619	1659	1739	1819	1859	1939	2019	2059	2139	2219	2259
Hooe Lake	......	......	......	......	......	......	......	......	......	......	1708	1748	1828	1908	1948	2028	2108	2148	2228	2308
Mount Batten (RAF Recpt)	1034	1114	1154	1234	1314	1354	1434	1514	1554	1634	1714	1754	1834	1914	1954	2034	2114	2154	2234	2322

SERVICE
MOUNT BATTEN - CATTEDOWN - CITY CENTRE - SALTASH PASSAGE 7

Via Church Hill, Hooe Road, Green Park Road, Goosewell Road, Dolphin Court Road, Dunstone Drive, Stanborough Road, Horn Cross Road, Pomphlett Road, Laira Bridge, Embankment Road, Elliott Road, South Milton Street, Commercial Road, Sutton Road, Exeter Street, Royal Parade, Union Street, Western Approach, Plymouth Station, Stuart Road, Wilton Street, Paradise Road, Fore Street, Park Avenue, Keyham Road, Saltash Road, Wolseley Road, Poole Park Road, Foulston Avenue, Rennie Avenue, Wolseley Road.

Sundays

Mount Batten (RAF Recpt)	0925	1005	1045	1125	1205	1245	1325	1405	1445	1525	1605	1645	1725	1805	1845	1925	2005	2045	2125	2200	2240	2326
Hooe Lake	0931	1011	1051	1131	1211	1251	1331	1411	1451	1531	1611	1651	1731	1811	1851	1931	2011	2051	2131	2206	2246	2332
Plymstock (Library)	0940	1020	1100	1140	1220	1300	1340	1420	1500	1540	1620	1700	1740	1820	1900	1940	2020	2100	2140	2215	2255	2341
Laira Bridge (W.N. Garage)	0946	1026	1106	1146	1226	1306	1346	1426	1506	1546	1626	1706	1746	1826	1906	1946	2026	2106	2146	2221	2301	2347
Royal Parade	0956	1036	1116	1156	1236	1316	1356	1436	1516	1556	1636	1716	1756	1836	1916	1956	2035	2116	2156	2231	......	......
Devonport (Granby Way)	1010	1050	1130	1210	1250	1330	1410	1450	1530	1610	1650	1730	1810	1850	1930	2010	2050	2130	2210	2245	......	......
St. Budeaux Square	1023	1103	1143	1223	1303	1343	1423	1503	1543	1623	1703	1743	1823	1903	1943	2023	2103	2143	2223	2258	......	......
Saltash Passage	1033	1113	1153	1233	1313	1353	1433	1513	1633	1713	1753	1833	1913	1963	2033	2113	2153	2233	2308	......	......	......

A general view of Friary Station after closure to passengers but prior to demolition of the goods shed. 5th May 1963.

S. C. Nash

A view of Friary Station in 1967, showing the new freight depot sheds and the then abandoned passenger station with its buildings fast becoming derelict.

Pamlin Prints

Plymouth Friary Station at commencement of its demolition. March 1976.

Author

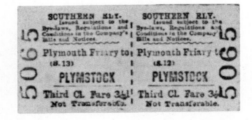

Friary Station site and Friary yard in their present day role as part of the new BR frieght handling complex with raod/rail transfer facilities for Roadline and other services. c1st May 1981.

Author

GOODS TRAFFIC ON THE BRANCHES AT THEIR ZENITH AND DURING LATER YEARS.

Incoming Traffic

PLYMSTOCK
Coal — Domestic for the Plymouth Co-operative Society.
Asphalt — Limmer & Trinidad Asphalt Co.
Timber — Cole Bros.
Liquid Petroleum Gas — Present day for the South Western Gas Board.

ORESTON
(F. J. Moore Ltd. private siding)
Coal — for Radford Quarry.
Paper sacks — ex Northfleet.
(Baylys private siding, Plymouth & Oreston Timber Co.)
Rail chairs — ex GKN Ltd. Cwmbran.
Sleepers and crossing timbers — ex Avonmouth and Millbay Docks.

TURNCHAPEL (WHARVES)
Admiralty stores — Naval Stores Office and Boom Defence Office.
(Pre World War I, general goods traffic for Messrs. Bulteel).

Outgoing Traffic

PLYMSTOCK
Cement — ex Associated Portland Cement Co. Ltd. works (Present day traffic).

ORESTON
(F. J. Moore Ltd. private siding).
Lime — Both packed and bulk for stations in Cornwall and North Devon. This was for building and agricultural use.
(Baylys private siding, Plymouth & Oreston Timber Co.)
GWR chaired sleepers and crossing for all stations west of Taunton. During latter years, most of this traffic was despatched to the GWR depot at Doublebois, Cornwall for preassembly.

TURNCHAPEL (WHARVES)
Admiralty stores - Naval Stores Office and Boom Defence Office.
Aviation fuel — for RAF bomber station (World War II).

Turnchapel swing bridge was opened frequently during the early days for sailing ships to load ballast to enable their return after unloading manure at Cattewater. In latter years however, it opened only for yachts and house boats.

When Turnchapel Station was destroyed by fire, following enemy action on 27th November 1941, passenger trains were terminated at Plymstock. Buses were used between Plymstock and Turnchapel. Freight trains continued to Bayly's siding with the Annett's Key. A Turnchapel tablet was kept in the safe at Plymstock to be issued to the driver, with the authority to proceed to Oreston, and shunt there within the private siding. A banner and detonators were placed at the Turnchapel end of Oreston Station prior to this movement. The tablet was returned to the safe at Plymstock on the train's return.

Incoming Traffic 1930s and 1960s

THE CATTEWATER BRANCH
Bitumen — S W Tar Distilleries.
General goods - Messrs. Court Lines Ltd.
Coal — Plymouth Corporation Electric Works.
Clay — English China Clay Co.
Chemicals — Fisons Ltd.
Steel — Blight and White Ltd.

Outgoing Traffic 1930s and 1960s

Oil — Anglo American; Regent; National Benzole; Shell Mex and B.P. Companies.
Lime and quarry stone — F. J. Moore Ltd.
General goods — Messrs. Court Lines Ltd.
Coal — John Wescott Ltd.
Fertiliser products — Fisons Ltd.
Tarmacadam — S W Tar Distilleries.
Finished steel products — Blight and White Ltd.
Scrap metal — Castles Shipbreaking Co.

Incoming Traffic surviving in 1980s

Bitumen — 2 trains weekly of 350 tons in 20 ton wagons — Esso Co.
Bulk Butane and Propane Gas — Shell Co.

Outgoing Traffic surviving in 1980s

Fertiliser products — Fisons Ltd. (1980 only).
Fuel for BR diesel motive power depots at Laira, Newton Abbot, St. Blazey and Penzance — Esso Co.

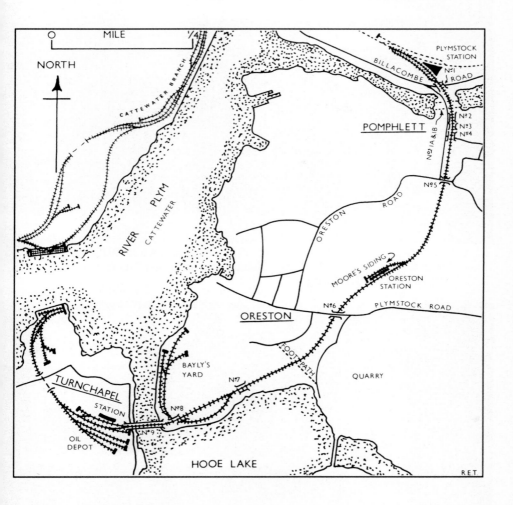

Map showing the relative routes of the Turnchapel and Cattewater branches on either side of the River Plym.

Members of LSWR staff outside the offices at Cattedown in 1922. They are Porter S. Lake; Clerk W. Lake; Shunter W. Saunders; Number Taker R. Bragg and Guard J. Ellacott.

Courtesy R. Bragg

Against the background of No. 11227, are ranged the crew and members of Plymstock Station staff. From left to right are:– Sig. J. Thomas; Driver D. Monk; Light Porter L. Summers; Goods Guard L. Jones and Relief Signalman T. Easton c20th October 1961.

W. E. Stevens

The interior of Plymstock Signal Box during 1961. Signalman J. Thomas is on duty.

W.E. Stevens

Plymstock Electric Train Tablet.

ENGINEERING AND OPERATING DATA

Pages 103 to 127 are reproduced from SWR Instructions Nos. 118/92; 116/92; 364/96; 44/97; 15/98 & 16/98.

Pages 128 to 133 are reproduced from SR General and Western Appendices to the Working Time Tables. From 26 March 1934 and until further notice.

Pages 134 to 135 are reproduced from SR Standard Regulations for Train Signalling. From 2 February 1930 on D & S lines, including revisions up until 1945.

Pages 136 to 139 are reproduced from the Sectional Appendix to Working Time Tables and Books of Rules and Regulations, British Railways (Western Region). Plymouth Traffic District, June 1960.

(Pages 103 to 139 inclusive are reproduced by kind permission of British Railways Board and, irrespective of dates, remain its exclusive copyright).

Pages 140 to 144 are signal box diagrams of stations/junctions applicable to both branches. They are specially prepared for this book by the Historical Signalling Society.

Pages 9, 77, 88, 89, 95, 102 & 131 carry photographs of luggage labels and passenger tickets used on the line.

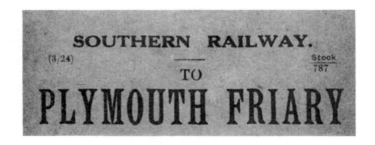

SOUTH WESTERN RAILWAY.

INSTRUCTION
No. 118, 1892.

OPENING of the PLYMSTOCK BRANCH LINE

AND

NEW AND ALTERED SIGNALS

IN CONNECTION THEREWITH

On MONDAY, 5th SEPTEMBER, 1892,

FOR PASSENGER, PARCELS AND GOODS TRAFFIC.

INSTRUCTIONS to Superintendents, Station Masters, Inspectors, Enginemen, Guards, Signalmen, and all others concerned.

STATION MASTERS are required personally to distribute this Notice to their Staff; and every person supplied with a copy is held responsible to read it carefully through, to note the general information it contains, and to act up to and obey the instructions particularly applicable to himself. No excuse of want of knowledge of these Special Arrangements can be admitted for any failure or neglect of duty.

The Plymstock Line runs out of the Cattewater Branch, at a spot 1,005 yards from the "A" Signal Box, Friary; it is about 1 mile in length and is nearly level throughout; it is a Single Line, and will be worked under the absolute Block System (Single wire) as described in Instruction No. 139, 1890.

The Line will also be worked by a Train Staff (see separate Instruction No. 116 on green paper).

The Service of Trains between Plymouth (Friary) and Plymstock on week-days will be as follows :—

FRIARY TO PLYMSTOCK.

	Pass. a.m.	Pass. a.m.	Goods. a.m.	Pass. a.m.	Pass. p.m.	Pass. p.m.	Pass. p.m.	Pass. p.m.	Pass. p.m.	
Plymouth (Friary) dep.	7 55	9 45	10 55	11 45	1 40	2 50	4 10	5 15	6 10	NO SUNDAY TRAINS.
Plymstock ... arr.	8 0	9 50	11 5	11 50	1 45	2 55	4 15	5 20	6 15	

PLYMSTOCK TO FRIARY.

	Pass. a.m.	Pass. a.m.	Goods. a.m.	Pass. p.m.	Pass. p.m.	Pass. p.m.	Pass. p.m.	Goods & Empty Coaches. p.m.	Pass. p.m.	
Plymstock ... dep.	8 15	10 30	11 15	12 20	2 0	3 45	4 40	5 25	6 40	NO SUNDAY TRAINS.
Plymouth (Friary) arr.	8 20	10 35	11 25	12 25	2 5	3 50	4 45	5 35	6 45	

FRIARY STATION.

New Signals have been erected as follows :—

A Four Arm Bracket Signal between the Station Siding and the Goods Departure Line.

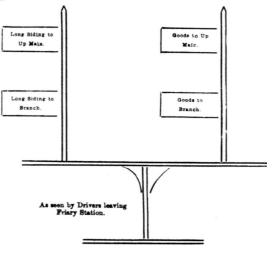

As seen by Drivers leaving
Friary Station.

A Four Arm Bracket Signal between the mileage road and the embankment.

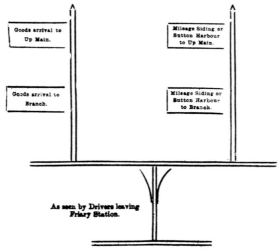

As seen by Drivers leaving
Friary Station.

FRIARY STATION— *continued.*

A Two Arm Signal at the Junction of the Plymstock Line with the Goods Yard for Trains from Plymstock going to Goods Yard or to the Long Siding.

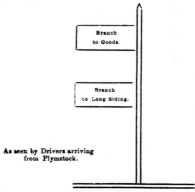

Branch to Goods.

Branch to Long Siding.

As seen by Drivers arriving from Plymstock.

There is a throw-off switch in the Goods and Plymstock Line at the fouling points of the Plymstock connection with the Down Main Line, and at this throw-off there is a **Ground Disc** which will control Trains or Engines shunting from the Goods Yard on to the Plymstock Branch Line.

A Semaphore Signal, which will be the **Starting Signal** for Trains going from the Goods Yard to the Branch Line, near the Ground Disc last mentioned.

A Semaphore Signal on the Branch Line about 288 yards ahead of the points connecting the Branch with the Up Main Line will be the **Advance Starting Signal** for all Trains going to Plymstock.

A Two Arm Bracket Signal on the Branch Line near the points connecting the Branch with the Up Main Line.

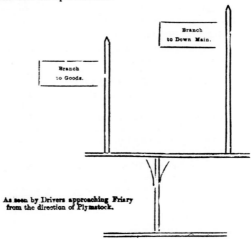

Branch to Down Main.

Branch to Goods.

As seen by Drivers approaching Friary from the direction of Plymstock.

FRIARY STATION—*continued.*

A Two Arm Bracket Signal at the Junction points in the Up Main Line.

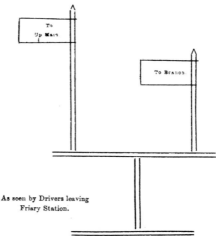

As seen by Drivers leaving
Friary Station.

All other Signals remain as at present.

PLYMSTOCK STATION.

A New Signal Box has been erected and the following Signals will be worked therefrom :—

A Distant Signal about 652 yards from the Signal Box, and about 607 yards from the Stop Signal, and will control Trains going to Plymstock.

A Stop Signal about 45 yards from the Signal Box.

A Starting Signal at the end of the Platform, and about 50 yards from the Signal Box, and will control Trains leaving Plymstock for Friary.

An Advance Starting Signal 286 yards from Signal Box.

Ground Discs have been fixed for shunting into and out of the Loop at the Station and into and out of the Loading Dock.

CATTEWATER BRANCH.

This Line branches off the Plymstock Line about 1,005 yards from the "A" Signal Box, Friary, and the Points (the normal position of which will be right for Plymstock Line) leading on to the Branch are fitted with an Annett's Lock, the key of which is the Plymstock Train Staff, and the Points cannot be moved until the Train Staff has been placed in the Annett's Lock and the Points unlocked.

After the Points are unlocked the Train Staff cannot be released until the Points have been put back to their normal position.

WATERLOO BRIDGE STATION,
30th *August,* 1892.
(A. 28,231.)   (2/36,270.)

E. W. VERRINDER.
(500)

Waterlow & Sons Limited, Printers, London Wall, London.

SOUTH WESTERN RAILWAY.

INSTRUCTION
No. 116, 1892.

PLYMOUTH (FRIARY) AND PLYMSTOCK LINE.

RULES FOR WORKING THE SINGLE LINE BETWEEN

PLYMOUTH (FRIARY) AND PLYMSTOCK

WITH TRAIN STAFF.

On and after Monday, 5th September, 1892.

---

1. The above-named Line will be worked with a Train Staff in one section, as follows :—

PLYMOUTH (FRIARY) **AND PLYMSTOCK.**

2. **The Train Staff is to be carried on the Engine of every Train or Engine to and fro, without which no Train or Engine is to be allowed to start.**

3. The person in charge of the Sectional Station for the time, is the *sole* person authorised to receive and deliver the Staff, and the Staff must be kept in the Station Master's office during the time Trains are not running.

4. An Engineman taking the Staff beyond the Sectional Station to which it belongs, or leaving a Sectional Station without the proper Staff, will subject himself to serious punishment although no accident may arise.

5. Enginemen are not to start from either of the Sectional Stations until the Guard has given the usual Signal and the Train Staff has been fixed in the proper place on the Engine.

6. A Guard is not to give his Driver a signal to start until he has seen the Train Staff in the possession of the Driver, and he will be held equally responsible with the Driver in the event of a Train starting without the Staff.

7. Special Trains, Ballast Trains, Light Engines, or Trains with stores or materials are to be treated in every respect like ordinary Passenger or Goods Trains, as regards the Staff arrangements.

8. **In case of any accident or extraordinary occurrence,** it may be necessary to make special arrangements for the working of the Single Line between Plymouth (Friary) and Plymstock. **Mr. Avery.** Plymouth **(Friary),** is the sole person who has authority to do so, and he will act according to the rules and regulations commencing at page 170 of the Book of Rules, dated 1st November, 1890, and Appendix, dated January, 1892.

By Order,

E. W. VERRINDER.

Traffic Superintendent's Office,
Waterloo Station, 30th August, 1892.

PLYMOUTH (Friary) AND PLYMSTOCK BRANCH LINE.

Special Instructions as to Electric Signalling between Friary and Plymstock, also Special Instructions as to Engine Whistle Codes, &c.

The Electric Bell Code for the Plymstock Trains between "A" and "B" Signal-boxes at Friary will be as follows :—

Warning Signal ● ● ● ● – ● ● ● ●
Departure Signal ● ● ● ●

The Bell-Code between Friary "A" Box and Plymstock will be in accordance with the Single Line Block Instructions, 139, dated 16th November, 1890, with the following exceptions :—

The Electric Signals at Plymstock worked from Friary "A" Box must be kept on except when lowered to allow a Train or Engine to leave Plymstock, they will be replaced at Danger as soon as the departure Signal has been received, and when the Train or Engine has passed out of the section, three beats on bell must be given to Plymstock, thus ● ● ● to inform the Signalman there that the Train has passed out of the section, so as to enable him to complete the record of it in the Train Signal Book.

All Trains or Engines going to Cattewater must be electrically signalled to Plymstock in the same way as if they were going to Plymstock and on the arrival of such Trains or Engine at "A" Box on the return journey from Cattewater, the line must be cleared to Plymstock by sending Error Signal.

ENGINE WHISTLE CODE.

FRIARY "A" SIGNAL BOX.

Up Main Line Trains or Engines	... One whistle.
Down Branch Trains or Engines, Friary to Plymstock	... Two whistles.
Engines from Engine Shed to Passenger Station ...	... Three whistles.
Down Main Line Passenger Trains or Engines ...	... One whistle.
Up Branch Passenger Trains from Plymstock ...	... Two whistles.
Down Main Line Goods Trains	... Three whistles.
Up Branch Goods Trains from Plymstock	... Four whistles.

FRIARY "B" SIGNAL BOX.

Up Trains starting from Friary Station will whistle according to the number of Line from which they start thus : from No. 4 road, four whistles, from No. 5 road, five whistles.

GOODS TRAINS OR ENGINES GOING TO THE CATTE-WATER BRANCH.

After the points have been unlocked by means of the Annett's Key attached to the Train Staff and the Train or Engine has passed on to the Cattewater Line clear

Goods Trains or Engines going to the Cattewater
Branch—*continued.*

of the throw-off switch, the points must be replaced in their normal position, and the Staff taken out and carried on the Engine whilst the Train or Engine is on the Cattewater Line.

After the work has been completed at Cattewater and the Train is ready to start for Friary, the Shunter will take the Staff from the Driver and unlock the points and set them right for the Train to go to Friary. On receipt of a Hand-Signal from the Shunter the Inspector in charge of Cattewater Branch will take off the Signal and the Guard will then give the Driver a signal to start, and when the load is heavy, will instruct him to run on to the level before stopping to pick up the Shunter, who, after closing and locking the points in their normal position, will take the Staff to the Driver.

Under no circumstances must the Driver of an Up Train from Cattewater pass the Stop Signal at Friary "A" Box until the Staff is in his possession.

PLYMSTOCK AND CATTEWATER BRANCH.

ENGINE CODE.

One Round White Disc centre of Smoke Box by day.
One White Light centre of Smoke Box by night.

SPECIAL INSTRUCTIONS TO THE SIGNALMEN AT FRIARY "A" BOX.

After a Down Train or Engine has left Friary Junction, no Train or Engine, going to Friary Passenger Station, must be permitted to come off the Plymstock Branch until after the Main Line Train or Engine has cleared back from Friary "B" Box.

(2/36,270.)

Traffic Superintendent's Office,
Waterloo Bridge Station,
20th September, 1892.

E. W. VERRINDER.

(1,500)

Waterlow & Sons Limited, Printers, London Wall, London.

SOUTH WESTERN RAILWAY.

INSTRUCTION
No. 364, 1896.

OPENING

THE

TURNCHAPEL BRANCH LINE

FOR

PASSENGER, PARCELS, AND GOODS TRAFFIC,

AND

NEW AND ALTERED SIGNALS

IN CONNECTION THEREWITH,

On *FRIDAY, JANUARY* 1st, 1897.

Instructions to District Superintendents, Station Masters, Inspectors, Enginemen, Guards, Signalmen, and all others concerned.

STATION MASTERS are required personally to distribute this Notice to their Staff; and every person supplied with a copy is held responsible to read it carefully through, to note the general information it contains, and to act up to and obey the instructions particularly applicable to himself. No excuse of want of knowledge of these Special Arrangements can be admitted for any failure or neglect of duty.

The Turnchapel Line runs out of the Plymstock Branch at the Western end of Plymstock Station; it is about 1 mile 6 chains in length; it is a Single Line, and will be worked in one section under Tyers' (New) Train Tablet system as described in Instruction No. 339, 1896.

This Tablet Instruction has been supplied to all concerned, including Enginemen and Guards, and must be exhibited in the Station Master's Offices and Signal Boxes at Plymstock and Turnchapel.

The Line rises slightly from Plymstock to Oreston and falls 1 in 50 for half a mile, then level for one furlong to end of Hooe Lake Bridge, and 1 in 80 thence to Turnchapel.

The gradients are as shown below :—

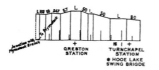

| The Engine Head Discs will be as under :—

The Service of Trains between Plymouth (Friary), Plymstock and Turnchapel on Week-days, will be as follows :— See Page 82

PLYMSTOCK STATION.

The following new Signals have been provided at Plymstock Station.

A two-armed bracket Post has been erected on the Down Line Side 800 yards from the Down Stop Signal towards Friary and will apply as shown on Diagram No. 1.

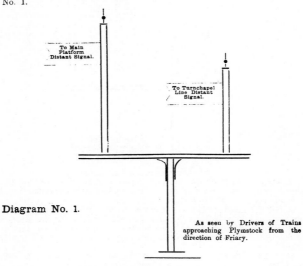

To Main
Platform
Distant Signal.

To Turnchapel
Line Distant
Signal.

Diagram No. 1.

As seen by Drivers of Trains approaching Plymstock from the direction of Friary.

A two-armed bracket Post has been erected on the Down Line Side about 200 yards from Plymstock Station which will apply as shown on Diagram No. 2.

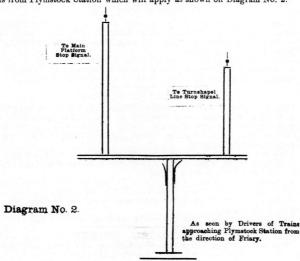

To Main
Platform
Stop Signal.

To Turnchapel
Line Stop Signal.

Diagram No. 2.

As seen by Drivers of Trains approaching Plymstock Station from the direction of Friary.

PLYMSTOCK STATION.—*continued.*

A two-armed bracket Post has been erected at the Friary end of the Platform, which will apply as shown on Diagram No. 3.

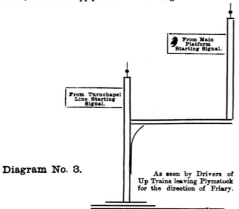

From Main
Platform
Starting Signal.

From Turnchapel
Line Starting
Signal.

Diagram No. 3.

As seen by Drivers of
Up Trains leaving Plymstock
for the direction of Friary.

A Single Arm Post has been erected at the Turnchapel end of the new Platform, and on the Down Line Side, which will be the **Down Starting Signal** for Trains going **to Turnchapel**.

A Single Arm Post has been erected on the Up Line Side on the Turnchapel Branch, about 210 yards from the Signal Box, which will be the **Up Stop Signal**.

A Single Arm Post has been erected on the Up Line Side on the Turnchapel Branch, about 800 yards from the Up Stop Signal, which will be the **Up Distant Signal**.

Ground Discs are provided for Shunting to and from the Sidings and Main Lines.

These Discs are for Shunting purposes only, and must not be taken for right-away Signals.

The Signal Box at **Plymstock** will be open from **7.0 a.m.** to **6.50 p.m.**

ORESTON STATION.

Oreston Station is situated half a mile from Plymstock, and has one Platform, 160 feet in length, with Waiting Shed and Booking Office on the right-hand side of the Line when travelling from Plymstock to Turnchapel.

Oreston has no Signals, and is not a Block Signalling Section.

All Passenger Trains will stop there to set down and take up Passengers.

Passenger and Parcels Traffic only will be dealt with at this Station.

TURNCHAPEL STATION.

There is one Platform at this Station, 175 feet in length.

A Signal Box has been erected on the Down Line Side at the Plymstock end of the Station, from which will be worked or controlled the Loop Points, Hooe Lake Swing Bridge and the undermentioned Signals.

This Signal Box will be open from 7.0 a.m. to 6.0 p.m.

A Single Arm Post on the Plymstock Side of the Hooe Lake Bridge will be the **"Inner" Down Stop Signal**.

A Single Arm Post, about 200 yards from the Inner Down Stop Signal towards Plymstock, will be the **"Outer" Down Stop Signal**.

A Single Arm Post, at the Plymstock end of the Platform, will be the **Up Starting Signal**.

Passenger and Parcels Traffic only will be dealt with at this Station.

TURNCHAPEL WHARF.

There are Sidings at Turnchapel Wharf, about 500 yards from Turnchapel Station, where Goods Traffic for Messrs. Bulteel will be dealt with.

SPECIAL ARRANGEMENTS AND INSTRUCTIONS.

RADFORD PUBLIC CROSSING.

This is a Public Footpath Crossing between Oreston and Turnchapel and an Electric Bell has been provided to warn the Public of the approach of **Down Trains,** the Bell is set in motion automatically by a Treadle at the Turnchapel end of Oreston Station.

BAYLY'S SIDING.

Bayly's Siding is situated about 300 yards from Turnchapel in the Plymstock and Turnchapel Train Tablet Section.

The Points leading into this Siding are facing for Down Trains, and their normal position will be right for the Main Line. They are fitted with an Annett's Lock and Key, and the Key is kept in the Locking Frame in the Plymstock Signal Box, interlocked with the Signals and cannot be released when a Train Tablet for the Plymstock and Turnchapel Section is out.

The Points cannot be moved until the Annett's Key has been placed in the Lock and the Points unlocked. After the Points are unlocked the Annett's Key cannot be withdrawn until the Points have been put back to their normal position and again locked; neither can a Train Tablet for the Section be obtained until the Annett's Key has been replaced in the Locking Frame in the Plymstock Signal Box.

The Station Master at Plymstock will be responsible for the working of this Siding, and when any Trucks have to be taken there, or any Trucks brought away, the Guard of the Train will obtain the Annett's Key from the Station Master at Plymstock Station and hand it to the Driver, and the Key, which has a brass plate affixed to it, lettered "For Bayly's Siding," is the Driver's authority for proceeding on to the Single Line from Plymstock to **Bayly's Siding and no farther.** On arrival at the Siding the Guard will take the Key from the Driver and place it in the Lock to release the Points, and after the necessary work has been done he will again lock the Points, and will return the Key to the Driver as his authority for returning on the Single Line from "Bayly's Siding" to Plymstock.

On arrival at Plymstock Station the Driver will again hand the Annett's Key to the Guard in charge of the Train, who will return it to the Station Master and the latter will have it replaced in the Locking Frame, and the ordinary working can then be resumed.

In foggy weather, before starting a Train from Plymstock for Bayly's Siding with the Annett's Key, the Station Master at Plymstock must send a competent man with two Fog Signals to be placed on the Rails at 100 and 110 yards from Bayly's Siding on the Plymstock side to warn the Driver that he is approaching the Siding.

Under no circumstances must the Annett's Key be replaced in the Frame in the Signal Box until the Train for which it was withdrawn has returned to Plymstock Station clear of the Section.

HOOE LAKE SWING BRIDGE.

This Bridge is situated between Plymstock and Turnchapel, about 60 yards from Turnchapel, and it has to be opened to allow vessels to pass. Its normal position will be "closed" by day and night.

The Signalman on duty in the Turnchapel Signal Box will be responsible for the opening and closing of the Bridge and he must always be present to superintend the opening, proper closing, bolting and locking of it. He must always have in his possession a Red Flag and a Hand Signal Lamp, also Fog Signals.

SPECIAL ARRANGEMENTS AND INSTRUCTIONS—*continued*

HOOE LAKE SWING BRIDGE—*continued.*

The Platelayers must always assist the Signalman, whenever called upon, in opening and closing the Bridge.

The Bridge must not be opened, when its opening may cause detention to a Train, and it must always be closed half an hour before a Train is due.

The Bridge is secured by means of a bolt worked from the Turnchapel Signal Box and this bolt is electrically locked from Plymstock Station. The Bridge Bolt cannot be released to unlock the Bridge whilst a Tablet for the Plymstock and Turnchapel Section is out, or the out-door Signals at Turnchapel or Plymstock are standing at off.

When the Bridge is open all the Electric Signalling communication between Plymstock and Turnchapel will be destroyed, and the out-door Signals at Turnchapel and Plymstock cannot be taken off or a Train Tablet for the Plymstock and Turnchapel Section obtained at either Signal Box.

The Bridge must only be opened by day or night by the direct permission of the Signalman on duty in the Turnchapel Signal Box.

The mode of opening and closing the Bridge will be as follows :—

By Day. Before the Bridge can be unlocked and permission given to open it by day the Signalman at Turnchapel must give eight beats, thus ●●●● pause ●●●● on the bell to Plymstock and this Signal must be repeated by the Signalman at Plymstock who, when repeating the Signal, must keep his Plunger pressed down for five seconds upon giving the last beat ; and the Signalman at Turnchapel, upon seeing the needle deflected, must press in his Bridge Plunger, which will release the Bridge Bolt and the Bridge can then be opened. When the Bridge has again been closed the Signalman at Turnchapel must give four beats to Plymstock, thus ●●●●, which must be repeated by Plymstock and the usual working can then be resumed.

By Night. After all Trains have ceased running on the Turnchapel Branch, and the Signalman at Plymstock and Turnchapel have exchanged the Closing Signal, the Signalman at Turnchapel must give the Bridge Opening Signal and the Signalman at Plymstock must release the Bridge Bolt in accordance with the working shown above, after which the Signalman at Turnchapel must immediately test his Bridge Bolt Lever to see that it is electrically unlocked ; he must, however, be careful to replace the Lever in its normal position and so relock the Bridge.

The Signalman at Turnchapel Station, responsible for opening and closing the Bridge by night, must be in attendance from one and half hours before to one and half hours after high tide.

Before electric working between Turnchapel and Plymstock is resumed the next morning, the Signalman taking duty in the Turnchapel Signal Box must personally see that the Bridge is properly closed, bolted and locked by means of the Bridge Bolt Lever in his Signal Box ; he will then give the " Bridge closed " Signal to Plymstock, which must be repeated by Plymstock and the electric working can then be commenced in the usual way by exchanging the Opening Signal.

SOUTH WESTERN RAILWAY.

PLYMSTOCK BRANCH LINE.

RULES FOR WORKING THE SINGLE LINE

BETWEEN

FRIARY AND PLYMSTOCK,

WITH TRAIN STAFF AND TICKET.

1. The above-named Line will be worked with Train Staff and Ticket in one section, as follows :—

FRIARY AND PLYMSTOCK.

2. **A Train Staff (or Train Ticket) is to be carried on the Engine of each Train to and fro, without which no Engine is to be allowed to start.**

3. No Engine or Train is to be permitted to leave either Friary or Plymstock unless the proper Staff for the portion of the Line over which it is to travel is then at the Station.

4. If no second Engine or Train is intended to follow, the Staff is to be given to the Driver, who will show it to the Guard, and then fix it in the place made for it on his Engine.

5. If another Engine or Train is intended to follow *before the Staff can be returned,* a Train Ticket, stating " *the Train Staff will follow,*" will be given to the Driver in charge of the leading Train, who will show it to the Guard, then fix it in its place on the Engine, the Staff itself being given to the Driver of the last Train or Engine; after which no other Engine or Train can leave the Sectional Station, under any circumstances whatever, until the return of the Staff.

6. Whenever any Train is started from Friary or Plymstock with a Train Ticket, the Staff for that section of the Line over which the Train is about to run must be shown to the Driver and Guard, both of whom are hereby instructed not to start until they have seen the Staff.

7. The Train Tickets are to be kept in a Box fastened by an inside spring ; the key to open the Box is the Train Staff, so that a Ticket cannot be obtained without the Train Staff. Only one Ticket is to be taken each time the Box is opened. (See also below as to Trains assisted by second Engine.)

8. The Train Staff Ticket Boxes and Tickets are painted or printed the respective colour for each Section as given above, this is to prevent mistakes at the Sectional Stations.

9. The Ticket Boxes are fixed by two brackets, in the office, the brackets being turned up at the end to receive the Train Staff when at the Station.

10. The Station Master, or person in charge of the Sectional Station for the time, is the *sole* person authorised to receive and deliver the Staff or Ticket.

11. An Engineman taking the Staff, or Ticket, beyond the Sectional Station to which it belongs, or leaving a Sectional Station without the proper Staff or Ticket, as hereinbefore explained, will subject himself to serious punishment, although no accident may arise.

12. Enginemen are not to start from any of the Sectional Stations until the Guard has given the usual Signal and the proper Train Staff or Train Ticket has been fixed in the proper place on the Engine.

13. A Guard is not to give his Driver a signal to start until he has seen the proper Train Staff, or Ticket, in the possession of the Driver, and he will be held equally responsible with the Driver in the event of a Train starting without the Staff or Ticket.

14. Special Trains, Ballast Trains, Light Engines, or Trains with stores or materials, are to be treated in every respect like ordinary Passenger or Goods Trains, as regards the Staff and Ticket arrangements, except as provided for in Rule 373, Page 177 of the New Rule Book, dated November, 1890, where Ballast Trains working between two Sections must be in possession of the Staff.

15. **In case of any accident or extraordinary occurrence,** it may be necessary to make special arrangements for the working of the Single Line between Friary and Plymstock. **Mr. Avery, Friary,** is the sole person who has authority to do so, and he will act according to the rules and regulations commencing at page 170 of the New Book of Rules, dated 1st November, 1890, and Appendix, dated January, 1892.

With reference to the above Instructions as to

THE TRAIN STAFF AND TICKETS,

it is necessary to provide for cases in which two Trains are working on the Branch, and one Train gets late, and in order to avoid detention to the other Train it becomes necessary to alter the proper meeting places.

The following Instructions are applicable to such a case :—

Example.—Assuming that a Down Train is timed to leave Friary at 1.50 p.m. to arrive at Plymstock to cross the 2.0 p.m. Up Train, but the former Train is late, the Station Master at Friary, having the Train Staff in his possession, will telegraph to the Station Master at Plymstock thus—S.P.G.

" Avery, } to { Canvin,
" Friary } to { Plymstock.

"The 1.50 p.m. Down Train from Friary is late, send the 2.0 p.m. Up Train from Plymstock on to Friary. I have Staff, and will hold it till the 2.0 p.m. Up Train arrives at Friary."

NOTE.—*This message must never be sent until the Station Master has taken such steps by putting on the Out-door Signals, &c., as will prevent the Train referred to from passing or leaving his Station.*

The Station Master at Plymstock will repeat this Message back to Friary and Friary will reply " Correct."

The Station Master at Plymstock will then give a crossing order, on the proper Green form, to the Guard of the 2.0 p.m. Up Train, to proceed to Friary to pass the 1.50 p.m. Down Train there, and the Guard will deliver the order to the Driver after reading it, and the Driver will deliver it up at Friary.

It must, however, be understood that the message upon which a Train is ordered as above to cross at a Sectional Station other than the proper Crossing Station, must proceed (that is, the message must proceed) from the Sectional Station at which the Staff, for the Section of line over which the alteration takes place, rests—that is to say, the Station Master who sends the message must hold the Staff in his possession for that section of line.

Each Station Master must keep himself informed how the Trains are running, and the Station Master in possession of the Train Staff will be responsible for altering the crossing places of Trains, when necessary. So as to avoid delay of Trains, Crossing orders must be avoided as much as possible by arranging the working of the Train Staff or Tickets to the running of Trains may require.

IMPORTANT NOTICE AS TO TRAINS ASSISTED BY SECOND ENGINE.

The Special Attention of all concerned is called to the following extract from the New Rule Book, issued 1st November, 1890, page 174, as to Trains assisted by Second Engine :—

369.—" When any Train is assisted by a second Engine in the front, and each Train has to carry the Staff, the first or leading Engine must carry the Ticket and the second Engine the Staff. In cases where the Train is to be followed by another Train or Engine, the second as well as the leading Engine must carry a Ticket, and when the assistant Engine is behind pushing the Train, the Train Engine must carry a Ticket and the assistant Engine the Staff, except in cases where the Train and assistant Engine are travelling over the entire length of the Section and have to be followed by another Train or Engine, when the Train and assistant Engine must each have a Ticket. When the assistant Engine is intended to return to the Station from which it started without running through the entire Section, it must always carry the Staff."

By Order, GEO. T. WHITE,
Superintendent of Line.

(SEE OTHER SIDE.)

SOUTH WESTERN RAILWAY.

INSTRUCTION
No. 44, 1897.

REVISED INSTRUCTIONS
AS TO
WORKING
OF THE
TURNCHAPEL BRANCH LINE.

Instructions to District Superintendents, Station Masters, Inspectors, Enginemen, Guards, Signalmen, and all others concerned.

STATION MASTERS are required personally to distribute this Notice to their Staff; and every person supplied with a copy is held responsible to read it carefully through, to note the general information it contains, and to act up to and obey the instructions particularly applicable to himself. No excuse of want of knowledge of these Special Arrangements can be admitted for any failure or neglect of duty.

For description of the Line and Stations, also for the **Time Table** and particulars of Outdoor Signals, see Instruction No. 364, dated December, 1896.

SPECIAL ARRANGEMENTS AND INSTRUCTIONS.

TURNCHAPEL WHARF.

There are Sidings at Turnchapel Wharf, about 500 yards from Turnchapel Station, where Goods Traffic for Messrs. Bulteel will be dealt with.

The load of a Goods Train between Plymstock and Turnchapel Wharf must not exceed 12 Wagons and 1 Van.

RADFORD PUBLIC CROSSING.

This is a Public Footpath Crossing between Oreston and Turnchapel and an Electric Bell has been provided to warn the Public of the approach of **Down** Trains, the Bell is set in motion automatically by a Treadle at the Turnchapel end of Oreston Station.

BAYLY'S SIDING.

Bayly's Siding is situated about 300 yards from Turnchapel in the Plymstock and Turnchapel Train Tablet Section.

SPECIAL ARRANGEMENTS AND INSTRUCTIONS—*continued.*

BAYLY'S SIDING—*continued.*

The Points leading into this Siding are facing for Down Trains, and their normal position will be right for the Main Line. They are fitted with an Annett's Lock and Key, and the Key is kept in the Locking Frame in the Plymstock Signal Box, interlocked with the Signals and cannot be released when a Train Tablet for the Plymstock and Turnchapel Section is out.

The Points cannot be moved until the Annett's Key has been placed in the Lock and the Points unlocked. After the Points are unlocked the Annett's Key cannot be withdrawn until the Points have been put back to their normal position and again locked; neither can a Train Tablet for the Section be obtained until the Annett's Key has been replaced in the Locking Frame in the Plymstock Signal Box.

The Station Master at Plymstock will be responsible for the working of this Siding, and when any Trucks have to be taken there, or any Trucks brought away, the Guard of the Train will obtain the Annett's Key from the Station Master at Plymstock Station and hand it to the Driver, and the Key, which has a brass plate affixed to it, lettered "For Bayly's Siding," is the Driver's authority for proceeding on to the Single Line from Plymstock to **Bayly's Siding and no farther.** On arrival at the Siding the Guard will take the Key from the Driver and place it in the Lock to release the Points, and after the necessary work has been done he will again lock the Points, and will return the Key to the Driver as his authority for returning on the Single Line from "Bayly's Siding" to Plymstock.

On arrival at Plymstock Station the Driver will again hand the Annett's Key to the Guard in charge of the Train, who will return it to the Station Master and the latter will have it replaced in the Locking Frame.

In foggy weather, before starting a Train from Plymstock for Bayly's Siding with the Annett's Key, the Station Master at Plymstock must send a competent man with two Fog Signals to be placed on the Rails at 100 and 110 yards from Bayly's Siding on the Plymstock side to warn the Driver that he is approaching the Siding.

Under no circumstances must the Annett's Key be replaced in the Frame in the Signal Box until the Train for which it was withdrawn has returned to Plymstock Station clear of the Section.

Trains going to Bayly's Siding **must approach the Siding cautiously and stop Dead before reaching the Points.**

A Break Van must always be the last Vehicle of a Train going to or returning from the Siding.

LOAD OF GOODS TRAINS.

The Load of Goods Trains between Plymstock and Bayly's Siding must not exceed 12 Wagons and 1 Van.

SPECIAL ARRANGEMENTS AND INSTRUCTIONS—*continued.*

HOOE LAKE SWING BRIDGE.

This Bridge is situated between Plymstock and Turnchapel, about 60 yards from Turnchapel, and it has to be opened to allow vessels to pass. Its normal position will be "closed" by day and night.

The Signalman on duty in the Turnchapel Signal Box will be responsible for the opening and closing of the Bridge and he must always be present to superintend the opening, proper closing, bolting and locking of it. He must always have in his possession a Red Flag and a Hand Signal Lamp, also Fog Signals.

The Platelayers must always assist the Signalman, whenever called upon, in opening and closing the Bridge.

The Bridge must not be opened, when its opening may cause detention to a Train, and it must always be closed half an hour before a Train is due.

The Bridge is secured by means of a bolt worked from the Turnchapel Signal Box and this bolt is electrically locked from Plymstock Station. The Bridge Bolt cannot be released to unlock the Bridge whilst a Tablet for the Plymstock and Turnchapel Section is out, or the out-door Signals at Turnchapel or Plymstock are standing at off.

When the Bridge is open all the Electric Signalling communication between Plymstock and Turnchapel will be destroyed, and the out-door Signals at Turnchapel and Plymstock cannot be taken off or a Train Tablet for the Plymstock and Turnchapel Section obtained at either Signal Box.

The Bridge must only be opened by day or night by the direct permission of the Signalman on duty in the Turnchapel Signal Box.

The Signalman at Turnchapel Station, responsible for opening and closing the Bridge by night, must be in attendance from one and half hours before to one and half hours after high tide.

TO OBTAIN BRIDGE BOLT AND ANNETT'S KEY.

By Day.—Before the Bridge can be unlocked and permission given to open it by day the Signalman at Turnchapel must give eight beats thus ● ● ● —● ● ● ● on the bell to Plymstock, and this Signal must be repeated by the Signalman at Plymstock, after which the Signalman at Turnchapel will ring One on the bell to Plymstock and keep his bell-plunger pressed down for five seconds. The Signalman at Plymstock on receiving this beat will depress "Sykes' releasing plunger for Annett's Key" which will free the Annett's Key and at the same time lock up the Tablet Instrument at Plymstock. The Signalman at Plymstock will next press down his bell-plunger for five seconds and at the same time plunge once steadily on Sykes' Instrument, and Turnchapel at the same time will press in his Sykes' releasing plunger. This operation will release the Bridge Bolt and lock up the Tablet Instrument at Turnchapel.

SPECIAL ARRANGEMENTS AND INSTRUCTIONS—*continued.*

When the Bridge has again been closed the Signalman at Turnchapel must lift the rod of Sykes' Instrument to " locked " and then give four beats to Plymstock thus ● ● ● ●. When the Annett's Key has been replaced in the frame provided for it at Plymstock the Signalman at Plymstock must also lift the rod of Sykes' Instrument and repeat the four beats to Turnchapel; this operation will lock the Bridge Bolt and the Annett's Key, and the ordinary working can then be resumed.

Whenever the Annett's Key is required and the Bridge is closed, the Signalman at Plymstock must give four beats thus ● — ● ● — ● on the bell to Turnchapel, and the operation for opening the Bridge and releasing the Annett's Key as shown above must be gone through; and when the Annett's Key has been returned to its frame in the Signal Box the same arrangement for locking up the Annett's Key and Bridge Bolt will also apply, after which the ordinary working can be resumed.

By Night.—After all Trains have ceased running on the Turnchapel Branch, and the Signalmen at Plymstock and Turnchapel have exchanged the Closing Signal, the Bridge Bolt must be released in accordance with the working shown above, after which the Signalman at Turnchapel must immediately test his Bridge Bolt Lever to see that it is electrically unlocked; he must, however, be careful to replace the Lever in its normal position and so relock the Bridge.

Before electric working between Turnchapel and Plymstock is resumed the next morning, the Signalman taking duty in the Turnchapel Signal Box must personally see that the Bridge is properly closed, bolted and locked by means of the Bridge Bolt Lever in his Signal Box; he will then give the " Bridge closed " Signal to Plymstock, which must be repeated by Plymstock and the electric working can then be commenced in the usual way by exchanging the Opening Signal.

The Lineman (whose name is Woolacott) for the Train Tablet Stations, at Plymstock and Turnchapel, lives at Tavistock, and upon any irregularity or failure of the instruments occurring he must be communicated with immediately. In addition to the Lineman at Tavistock being advised, a wire must also be sent to **Mr. Avery, Friary, Mr. Watkins, Exeter,** and to **Mr. Vallance, Exeter,** giving particulars of the irregularity or failure, but the first care must be to secure the attendance of the resident Lineman, who must always leave word with the Station Master at Tavistock where he is to be found.

GEO. T. WHITE,

Waterloo Station,   *Superintendent of the Line.*

February 26th, 1897.

(A. 1/16,474. T.R.) (B. 2/94,731.) (1,800.)

Waterlow and Sons Limited, Printers, London Wall, London.

LONDON & SOUTH WESTERN RAILWAY.

INSTRUCTION No. 15, 1898.

Instructions to District Superintendents, Station Masters, Inspectors, Enginemen, Guards, Signalmen, and all others concerned,

FOR WORKING THE SINGLE LINE

ON THE

CATTEWATER BRANCH

WITH

TRAIN STAFF,

Commencing on THURSDAY, JANUARY 13th, 1898.

Only one Engine in Steam must be allowed to be on the Cattewater Branch at one time.

---

1. This Branch will be worked under the absolute Train Staff system as follows :—

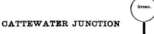

CATTEWATER JUNCTION and CATTEWATER BRANCH.

2. The Train Staff is to be carried on the Engine of every Train, or on every Light Engine running on the Branch, and without the Staff no Train or Engine is to be allowed to leave the Signal Box at Cattewater Junction for the Cattewater Branch.

3. When the Train or Engine returns to the Cattewater Junction Signal Box after having completed its work on the Cattewater Branch the Staff must be handed back to the Signalman.

4. The Signalman at the Cattewater Junction Box for the time is the **sole** person authorised to deliver and receive the Staff, and the Staff must be kept in the Signal Box during the time Trains are not running.

5. An Engineman entering the Cattewater Branch without the Train Staff, or taking the Staff beyond the Cattewater Junction Signal Box when leaving the Branch, will subject himself to serious punishment although no accident may arise.

6. Enginemen are not to start from Cattewater Junction Signal Box for the Cattewater Branch until the Guard has given the usual Signal and the Train Staff has been fixed in the proper place on the Engine.

7. A Guard must not give the Driver a signal to start from Cattewater Junction Signal Box, for the Cattewater Branch, until he has seen the Train Staff in the possession of the Driver, and he will be held equally responsible with the Driver in the event of a Train starting without the Staff.

8. Enginemen are not to proceed beyond Cattewater Junction Box on the return journey until the Train Staff has been handed back to the Signalman, and the Guard has given the usual Signal to start.

9. A Guard must not give the Driver a Signal to start from the Cattewater Junction Box on the return journey until he has seen the Train Staff in the possession of the Signalman, and he will be held equally responsible with the Driver in the event of a train leaving without the Train Staff having been returned to the Signalman.

10. Special Trains, Ballast Trains, Light Engines or Trains with stores or materials, are to be treated in every respect like ordinary Trains as regards the Staff arrangements.

11. **In case of any accident or extraordinary occurrence**, it may be necessary to make special arrangements for the working of the Single Line on the Cattewater Branch. **Mr. Avery, Friary,** is the sole person who has authority to do so, and he will act according to the rules and regulations commencing at page 155 of the Book of Rules, dated 1st November 1897, and Appendix, dated January, 1892.

WATERLOO STATION,
JANUARY 11th, 1898.
(T.R. 6/74,409.) (2/89,580)

GEO. T. WHITE,
Superintendent of the Line.
(1,800.)

Waterlow & Sons Limited, Printers, London Wall, London.

LONDON & SOUTH WESTERN RAILWAY.

INSTRUCTION No. 16, 1898.

OPENING of a NEW SIGNAL BOX
AT
CATTEWATER JUNCTION,
WITH NEW AND ALTERED SIGNALS,
On THURSDAY, JANUARY 13th, 1898.
ALSO
OPENING of the SOUTH HAMS RAILWAY,
AND BRINGING INTO USE THE
NEW AND ALTERED SIGNALS
IN CONNECTION THEREWITH,
On SATURDAY, JANUARY 15th, 1898.

Instructions to District Superintendents, Station Masters, Inspectors, Enginemen, Guards, Signalmen, and all others concerned.

STATION MASTERS are required personally to distribute this Notice to their Staff; and every person supplied with a copy is held responsible to read it carefully through, to note the general information it contains, and to act up to and obey the instructions particularly applicable to himself. No excuse of want of knowledge of these Special Arrangements can be admitted for any failure or neglect of duty.

The South Hams Railway will be opened to the public on Monday, January 17th, when the Service of Trains contained in this Notice will commence, but Passenger Trains in connection with the opening ceremony will run over the Line on Saturday, 15th January.

The South Hams Railway runs out of the Eastern end of Plymstock Station and it will be worked by the Great Western Railway Company.

The Line is 6¼ miles in length from Plymstock to Yealmpton, and there will be Stations at Billacombe, Elburton, Brixton Road, Steer Point and Yealmpton.

The Line from Plymstock to Yealmpton will be worked under the Electric Train Staff System.

The Great Western Company's Trains to and from Yealmpton will run over a New Curve Line which the Great Western Company have constructed between Mount Gould Junction and Cattewater Junction, passing thence over this Company's Line between Cattewater Junction and Plymstock.

CATTEWATER JUNCTION.

A New Signal Box has been erected on the Up Line side at Cattewater Junction, and in preparation for the opening of the New Line this Box will be brought into use commencing Thursday, January 13th, and out-door Signals will be worked therefrom, as shown in the following list.

A Three-armed bracket Signal on the Down Line side, 640 yards from the Signal Box towards Friary, which will apply as shown on Diagram No. 1.

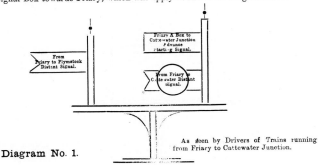

From Friary to Plymstock Distant Signal.

Friary A Box to Cattewater Junction Advance Starting Signal.

From Friary to Cattewater Distant signal.

As seen by Drivers of Trains running from Friary to Cattewater Junction.

Diagram No. 1.

CATTEWATER JUNCTION.
NEW AND ALTERED SIGNALS —*continued.*
To be brought into use on **Thursday, January 13th.**

A two-armed bracket Signal Post on the Down Line side, 180 yards the Friary side of the Cattewater Junction Signal Box. See Diagram No. 2.

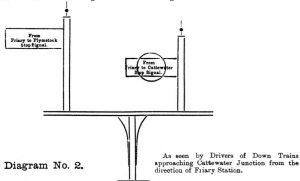

Diagram No. 2.

As seen by Drivers of Down Trains approaching Cattewater Junction from the direction of Friary Station.

The **Distant Signals** for trains to Plymstock and Cattewater from the Great Western Line are on the **Mount Gould Junction Starting Signal Post.** See Diagram No. 3.

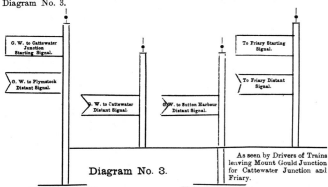

Diagram No. 3.

As seen by Drivers of Trains leaving Mount Gould Junction for Cattewater Junction and Friary.

A two-armed bracket Signal Post on the Great Western Line, 88 yards from Cattewater Junction Signal Box towards Mount Gould Junction will apply as shown on Diagram No. 4.

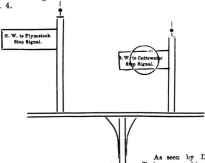

Diagram No. 4.

As seen by Drivers of Great Western Trains approaching Cattewater Junction from the direction of Mount Gould Junction.

CATTEWATER JUNCTION.
NEW AND ALTERED SIGNALS—*continued.*

To be brought into use on **Thursday, January 13th.**

A three-armed bracket Signal Post on the Plymstock Line, 285 yards from Cattewater Junction Signal Box, will apply as shown on Diagram No. 5.

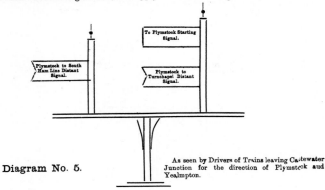

Diagram No. 5.

As seen by Drivers of Trains leaving Cattewater Junction for the direction of Plymstock and Yealmpton.

A two-armed Signal Post on the South Western Line, 197 yards from Cattewater Junction Signal Box towards Friary, will apply as shown on Diagram No. 6.

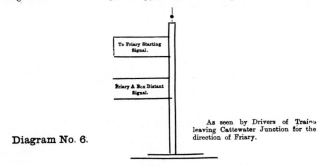

Diagram No. 6.

As seen by Drivers of Trains leaving Cattewater Junction for the direction of Friary.

A two-armed Signal on the Great Western Line, for Great Western Trains leaving Cattewater Junction in the direction of Mount Gould Junction, about 260 yards from Cattewater Junction Signal Box towards Mount Gould Junction, will apply as shown on Diagram No. 7.

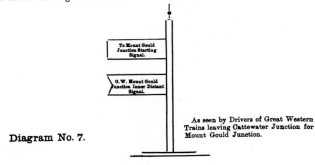

Diagram No. 7.

As seen by Drivers of Great Western Trains leaving Cattewater Junction for Mount Gould Junction.

CATTEWATER JUNCTION.
NEW AND ALTERED SIGNALS—*continued.*

To be brought into use on **Thursday, January 13th.**

A three-armed bracket Signal on the Cattewater Line, 128 yards from Cattewater Junction Signal Box, will apply as shown on Diagram No. 8.

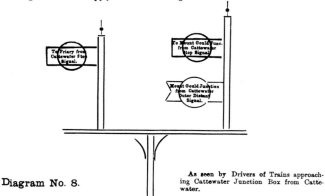

Diagram No. 8.

As seen by Drivers of Trains approaching Cattewater Junction Box from Cattewater.

A two-armed bracket Signal on the Cattewater Line, 150 yards from the Stop Signals, will apply as shown on Diagram No. 9.

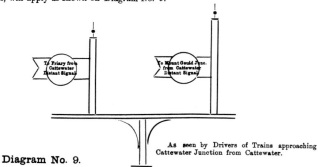

Diagram No. 9.

As seen by Drivers of Trains approaching Cattewater Junction from Cattewater.

A three-armed bracket Signal Post on the Plymstock Line, 190 yards from Cattewater Signal Box towards Plymstock, will apply as shown on Diagram No. 10.

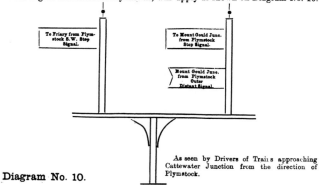

Diagram No. 10.

As seen by Drivers of Trains approaching Cattewater Junction from the direction of Plymstock.

CATTEWATER JUNCTION.

NEW AND ALTERED SIGNALS—*continued.*

To be brought into use on **Thursday, January 13th**.

A three-armed bracket Signal Post on the Plymstock Line, 573 yards from Cattewater Junction Stop Signals, and 289 yards the Cattewater Junction side of Plymstock Signal Box. See Diagram No. 11.

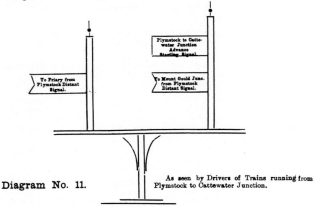

Diagram No. 11.

As seen by Drivers of Trains running from Plymstock to Cattewater Junction.

FRIARY " A " SIGNAL BOX.

The new **Distant Signal** for trains from Cattewater Junction is on the Cattewater Junction Starting Signal Post. See Diagram No. 6.

The new **Advance Starting Signal** for trains going towards Cattewater Junction is on the Cattewater Junction Distant Post. See Diagram No. 1.

SIGNALS TO BE REMOVED.

The existing Advance Starting Signal to Plymstock and Cattewater.

The existing Distant Signal from Plymstock and Cattewater.

PLYMSTOCK STATION.

New and **Altered Signals.** To be brought into use on **Thursday, January 13th**.

A **Starting Signal** has been provided at the Yealmpton end of the platform for trains going to Yealmpton.

The **Facing Points** at the Yealmpton end of the Station have been moved to a point about 60 feet nearer Yealmpton.

A **Stop Signal** has been provided for Up Yealmpton Trains about 135 yards from the Signal Box, and close to the above mentioned facing Points.

A **Distant Signal** has been provided for Up Yealmpton Line Trains about 900 yards from the Up Stop Signal.

The new **Up Advance Starting Signal** is on the Cattewater Junction Distant Signal Post. See Diagram No. 11.

The **Down Distant Signals** are on the Cattewater Junction Starting Post. See Diagram No. 5.

SIGNALS TO BE REMOVED.

The existing Up Advance Starting Signal.

The existing Down Distant Signals.

In connection with the opening of the South Hams Railway, the Train Staff and Ticket arrangements between Friary "A" Box and Plymstock will be abolished, and the Line between Friary "A" Box and **Plymstock** will be worked under **Tyers** (New) **Train Tablet System** as described in Instruction No. 17, 1898.

This Tablet Instruction will be supplied to all concerned, including Enginemen and Guards, and must be exhibited in the Station Master's Offices at Friary and Plymstock, also in Friary "A," Cattewater Junction and Plymstock Signal Boxes.

The **Train Tablet sections** will be as follows:

> **Friary "A" Box and Cattewater Junction.**
> **Cattewater Junction and Plymstock.**

Instructions as to Single Line Working by a Pilotman on Lines during the failure or breakdown of Tablet System:—

The working of the Traffic on Single Lines during a failure or breakdown of the Tablet Instruments, **when the Telegraph Speaking Instruments are not affected, must be by means of a Pilotman,** which is the only method sanctioned by the Board of Trade.

In order to minimise the delay to traffic, which must almost necessarily follow a breakdown, the method of establishing Pilot-working when only the Tablet Apparatus has failed will be different (with certain exceptions) to that when both the Tablet Apparatus and the Telegraph Speaking Instruments also have failed, according to the following particulars.

For example, assume that a Tablet cannot be obtained for a Down Train to proceed from Cattewater Junction to Plymstock.

FAILURE OF TABLET INSTRUMENT ONLY.

The Signalman at Cattewater Junction to immediately telegraph to the Station Master at Plymstock advising him of the failure and requesting him to establish Pilot-working for the Down Train, by filling in the necessary Pilot-working forms and sending a Pilotman as quickly as possible along the line (to ascertain that the section is clear) to Cattewater Junction.

FAILURE OF TABLET AND SPEAKING INSTRUMENTS.

The working must be in accordance with the following, viz.:—

The Station Master at Plymstock (having an Up Train to proceed to Cattewater Junction and being unable to obtain a Tablet) would fill in the requisite forms for Pilot-working and must himself proceed (or send a duly appointed Pilotman) to Cattewater Junction, and having left the necessary forms at the Signal Box there and ascertained that the Section is clear, return as quickly as possible to Plymstock Station for the Up Train.

Should it be expected that a Down Train would be due to leave Cattewater Junction during the interval that the Up Train would be detained at Plymstock, and which would enable the Pilotman to reach Plymstock sooner than by walking the distance or by conveyance, it would be his duty to wait and Pilot the Down Train.

These instructions apply to any two Tablet Stations and it is thus evident that the responsibility for safe working rests entirely with the Station Masters without communicating with a Crossing Agent, which cancels previous orders as to Crossing Agents on the Friary and Plymstock Line.

The Lineman for the Train Tablet Stations, Friary "A" Box to Plymstock inclusive, whose name is Woollacott, lives at Tavistock, and upon any irregularity or failure of the instruments occurring he must be communicated with immediately. In addition to the Lineman at Tavistock being advised, a wire must also be sent to **Mr. Watkins, Exeter,** and to **Mr. Vallance, Exeter,** giving particulars of the irregularity or failure, but the first care must be to secure the attendance of the resident Lineman, who must always leave word with the Station Master at Tavistock where he is to be found.

FRIARY "A" BOX AND CATTEWATER JUNCTION.

All Trains **must** slacken at Friary "A" Box and Cattewater Junction to receive or deliver up the **Train Tablet.**

CATTEWATER BRANCH.

On and after Thursday, January 13th, 1898, the Cattewater Branch will be worked under the **Absolute Train Staff System.** For full particulars see Instruction No. 15, 1898.

Commencing on **Monday, January 17th, 1898,** the Great Western Company's service of trains between Plymouth and Yealmpton will be as follows:—

STATIONS.	1 Passenger.		2 Goods.		3 Passenger.		4 Passenger.		5 Passenger.	
	arr. a.m.	dep. a.m.	arr. a.m.	dep. a.m.	arr. a.m.	dep. a.m.	arr. p.m.	dep. p.m.	arr. p.m.	dep. p.m.
Plymouth (Millbay)	...	6 55	...	...	...	9 45	...	1 5	...	6 0
Plymouth (North Road)	6 58	7 0	...	...	9 48	9 50	1 8	1 10	6 3	6 5
Mutley	7 1	7 3	...	...	9 51	9 53	1 11	1 13	6 6	6 8
Laira Junction	...	...	...	8 30	...	...	...	...	...	...
Cattewater Junction	7	9	8	33	9	59	1	19	6	14
Plymstock	7 11	7 13	8 35	8 50	10 1	10 3	1 21	1 23	6 16	6 18
Billacombe	7 16	7 18	8 55	9 2	10 6	10 8	1 26	1 28	6 21	6 23
Elburton	CR	7 23	...	...	CR	10 13	CR	1 33	...	...
Brixton Road	7 25	7 27	9 10	9 25	10 15	10 17	1 35	1 37	6 30	6 32
Sheer Point	7 30	7 32	9 30	9 40	10 20	10 22	1 40	1 42	6 35	6 37
Yealmpton	7 38	...	9 50	...	10 28	...	1 48	...	6 43	...

STATIONS.	1 Passenger.		2 Passenger.		3 Goods.		4 Passenger.		5 Passenger.	
	arr. a.m.	dep. a.m.	arr. a.m.	dep. a.m.	arr. a.m.	dep. a.m.	arr. p.m.	dep. p.m.	arr. p.m.	dep. p.m.
Yealmpton	...	7 50	...	10 55	...	11 25	...	2 30	...	7 5
Steer Point	7 56	7 58	11 1	11 3	11 35	11 45	2 36	2 38	7 11	7 13
Brixton Road	8 1	8 3	11 6	11 8	11 50	12 5	2 41	2 43	7 16	7 18
Elburton	CR	8 7	CR	11 12	...	...	CR	2 47	...	...
Billacombe	8 9	8 11	11 14	11 16	12 15	12 45	2 49	2 51	7 24	7 26
Plymstock	8 14	8 16	11 19	11 21	12 30	12 45	2 54	2 56	7 29	7 31
Cattewater Junction	8	18	11	23	12	47	2	58	7	33
Laira Junction	...	...	...	...	12 50	...	...	...	...	...
Mutley	8 24	8 26	11 29	11 31	...	...	3 4	3 6	7 39	7 41
Plymouth (North Road)	8 27	8 30	11 32	11 35	...	...	3 7	3 10	7 42	7 45
Plymouth (Millbay)	8 35	...	11 40	...	...	...	3 15	...	7 50	...

CR—Calls at Elburton when required.

Page 124 of the Main Line Service Book, so far as it relates to the Friary, Cattewater, Plymstock and Turnchapel Branches, will be re-issued for the opening of the South Hams Railway.

The **District Inspector** to report to me, through the District Superintendent, on the working of the New and Altered Signals.

WATERLOO STATION,
January 11th, 1898.
(A. 18,048.) (3/22099.)

GEO. T. WHITE,
Superintendent of the Line.
(2,000.)

Waterlow and Sons Limited, Printers, London Wall, London.

Working of pull and push trains without a Guard.—A junior Porter will accompany the train between Lucas Terrace Halt and Turnchapel to issue and collect tickets as may be necessary, and to perform the work of a platform Porter at Lucas Terrace Halt and at those stations where the train is booked to call but no platform staff are on duty. The junior Porter will also be responsible at Lucas Terrace Halt and such stations for giving the signal to the Driver to indicate that the platform work is completed and all is right for the train to proceed. He will undertake no responsibility appertaining to the actual running of the train.

Bayly's (Plymouth and Oreston Timber Co.) siding.—The points leading to the siding are facing for down trains. They are fitted with an Annett's lock and key, and the key is kept in the frame in Plymstock signal box, interlocked with the signals and tablet instrument, and cannot be released when a train tablet for the Plymstock-Turnchapel section is out of the instrument.

The Station Master at Plymouth Friary will be responsible for the safe working of this siding, which will be conducted by the Guard of the train, and when any wagons have to be taken there, or brought away, the Signalman at Plymstock station will hand the Annett's key to the Driver. This key, which has a brass plate affixed to it lettered " For Bayly's siding," is the Driver's authority for proceeding on to the single line from Plymstock to Bayly's siding and no further.

The train must come to a stand at a point just on the Turnchapel side of the platform at Oreston station, before reaching the falling gradient, to enable a sufficient number of wagon brakes to be securely applied by the Guard for safely controlling the train down the falling gradients towards and into Bayly's siding. The Guard must inform the Driver the number and class of vehicles forming the train, and agree with him the number of wagon brakes it is necessary to apply in order that the train may be brought to a stand by means of the combined brake power available on any portion of the falling gradients.

The train must stop clear of the siding points where it will be met by the man in charge at Oreston who will take the key from the Driver, release the points, admit the train to the siding, relock the points and then return the key to the Driver. He will accompany the train to the Plymouth and Oreston Timber Co's yard, and when it is ready to leave there, he will obtain the key from the Driver, release the points, and after the train has passed on to the single line, re-lock the points and hand the key to the Driver as his authority for returning on the single line to Plymstock.

On the return of the train to Plymstock the Driver will return the key to the Signalman, who must replace it in the locking frame.

In foggy weather, before starting a train from Plymstock for Bayly's siding with the Annett's key, the Signalman at Plymstock must request by telephone the man in charge at Oreston to place two detonators on the rails at 100 and 110 yards respectively from Bayly's siding, on the Plymstock side, to warn the Driver that he is approaching the siding.

Under no circumstances must the Annett's key be replaced in the frame in the signal box until the train for which it was withdrawn has returned to Plymstock station clear of the section.

A brake van must always be the last vehicle of a train going to or returning from the siding.

The Company's engine is prohibited from passing the gantry which is erected alongside, and over, the loop sidings at a point opposite the premises of the Plymouth and Oreston Timber Company.

Only goods vans which are not fitted with a stove must be permitted to work over this siding, as there is insufficient clearance under the gantry referred to in the preceding paragraph for a stove pipe to pass with safety.

Admiralty wharves.—When a train requires to run on to the Admiralty wharves at Turnchapel, the Porter Signalman at Turnchapel must first proceed to the wharves, obtain permission from the Admiralty authorities there for it to do so, and arrange for the gates across the single line, which are situated about 200 yards from the Turnchapel station, to be opened. He will then return to the station and accompany the train to the wharves, taking care that sufficient brake power is applied to safely control it.

Loads of goods trains between Plymstock and Turnchapel.—The load of a goods train between Plymstock and Turnchapel (wharf) must not exceed equal to 12 loaded goods wagons and one van, and between Plymstock and Bayly's siding must not exceed equal to 10 loaded goods wagons and one van.

CATTEWATER BRANCH.

This branch, which is connected with the Turnchapel Branch at Cattewater Junction, is worked as an ordinary shunting yard. One or more engines may be permitted on the branch at one time, as ordered by the Station Master at Plymouth Friary, who will provide a competent Shunter to take charge of, and remain with, each engine during the time it is engaged on the branch.

Shunters must be careful to see that engines are moved cautiously, and at a low speed, from one part of the Cattewater line to another ; must satisfy themselves, before allowing the trains to be moved, that the lines are clear for their passage, and must at all times keep a careful look-out for other trains, and shunting operations, and see that the several level crossings on the branch are clear.

The load of a train from Plymouth Friary to Cattewater must not exceed 60 wagons and one brake van ; and from Cattewater to Plymouth Friary the load must not exceed equal to 30 loaded goods wagons and one brake van.

The passage of trains between Cattewater Junction and Prince Rock level crossing is controlled by means of bell signals between those points.

The gates fencing the China Clay Company's tram line, which crosses the branch line on the level at a point adjacent to Prince Rock level crossing, must be placed across the tram line and the gates of the Prince Rock level crossing must be placed across the roadway; the respective gates must be secured in that position by padlocks before permission is given for a train to enter or leave the Cattewater Branch.

The gates at Cattedown level crossing, which fence the railway on the Cattewater Junction side only, must be kept normally closed across the railway and secured in that position by a padlock.

The Shunter in charge will be held responsible for seeing that the gates are opened and closed as required in connection with shunting operations.

Cattedown Wharves.—The connection leading to the siding nearest the warehouses is laid to a sharp curve and should it be necessary to work a bogie bolster wagon (or other similar vehicle) thereover, it must not be attached to other vehicles.

S.W. Tar Distilleries siding.—This siding is connected to the Cattewater line by hand points facing for trains from the direction of Cattewater Junction.

A tractor is in use by the Distilleries Coy. for the purpose of hauling wagons to and from their siding, and to place wagons in position alongside their premises on the Cattewater line.

The employees of the Distilleries Coy., before moving any wagons by means of the tractor, must obtain permission from the Inspector in charge of traffic working at Cattewater, and must keep the tractor clear of the Cattewater line during the time movements of the Railway Company's engines and vehicles are required to be made.

Anglo American Oil Co's and Moore's sidings.—The entrance to the sidings is laid on a severe right hand curve and passes across the roadway running alongside the east siding leading to Victoria Wharves and through a narrow passage cut through the rock cliff on the further side of the roadway.

At a short distance from the entrance to the siding, hand points exist leading to three separate sidings in the Anglo American Oil Company's premises, and a further set of hand points in the southernmost of these three sidings forms a connection to an intermediate siding between the southern and middle sidings. Staging exists alongside the intermediate siding for the accommodation of the Oil Company's filling plant, which staging is not of standard clearance from the near siding rail, and a notice board is exhibited near the entrance to the siding, beyond which board engines and high sided wagons must not proceed.

The middle siding extends to Messrs. F. J. Moore's lime kilns and quarries.

Shunting operations are carried out in charge of a competent man deputed by the Inspector at Cattewater.

Owing to the severe nature of the curve at the entrance to the sidings, and the difficulty of obtaining a clear view of the sidings from that point, it is necessary that movements into the sidings should be carried out with the utmost care, and the competent man in charge of shunting operations must satisfy himself before making movements into the siding that the line is clear to the point to which such operations are required to proceed.

Victoria Wharves sidings.—These two sidings form the terminal point of the Cattewater Branch, the Company's boundary being indicated approximately by a wall, office and weighbridge, the property of Messrs. Coast Lines Limited, who are the wharf owners.

Hand points situated approximately 100 yards on the Cattewater Junction side of the boundary, lead out of the west road of the Company's terminal loop, and serve the east siding leading to Victoria Wharves. The west siding is an extension of the loop road.

An overhead conveyor is provided over the loop roads, at the Cattewater Junction end at Victoria Wharves, and a chute which is operated by Messrs. John Westcott Ltd., is attached to the conveyor and, when lowered, fouls both the construction and load gauges.

Before movements are made by the Company's engine and vehicles over the right hand loop road, the Shunter in charge must obtain an assurance from Messrs. Westcott's Foreman, that the conveyor will not be set in motion over the sidings during the progress of the shunting movement.

Ingoing wagons for Victoria Wharves will usually be placed by the Company's engine on the east siding.

Outgoing wagons will usually be accepted on the west siding immediately inside the boundary gate. The Company's engine may proceed into the west siding for a distance of 30 yards on the right-hand loop road.

Shunting operations will be in charge of a competent man, deputed by the Inspector at Cattewater, and no movements on to the east or west sidings must be made until the competent man has satisfied himself that the line is clear and has come to an understanding with the wharf owners' employees in regard thereto.

The wharf owners' private locomotives are employed in the sidings and on the wharves for the purpose of making internal shunt movements, and such locomotives may be allowed to proceed from the west siding on to the Company's property for a short distance towards the terminal loop, if the line is clear, up to a point where a notice board is fixed. The wharf owners' private locomotives must not proceed from the east siding on to the Company's property beyond the boundary gate.

PULL AND PUSH TRAINS.

General instructions.—All pull and push services operating on the Southern Railway are worked by vehicles fitted with the vacuum brake, supplemented by air control for the engine regulator.

(1) Engines and coaches allocated to work in pull and push services are, in addition to the usual vacuum brake and steam heating pipes, fitted with :—

(a) Regulator control hose pipe (painted blue).
(b) Main storage hose pipe (painted green).
(c) Back pressure hose pipe (painted yellow).

(d) Cable with three pin coupler containing regulator indicator and bell wires providing bell communication between the driving cab of the engine and the driving compartment of the pull and push coach.

(e) Earth wire.

In addition to the pipes being specially coloured the designation of each is indicated adjacently on the head stock of the engine and the vehicles, and care must be taken by the staff concerned to see that the various connections are properly coupled. Enginemen will be responsible for seeing that this is done before commencing a journey.

NOTE.—The cocks on regulator control, main storage and back pressure pipes are open when the handles are standing at RIGHT ANGLES to the pipes.

(2) Certain pull and push engines are fitted with the Westinghouse brake which operates on the engine only, and the vacuum brake which operates on the coaches. Drivers of such engines must see that the regulations in regard to both vacuum and Westinghouse brakes are observed.

(3) As a principle not more than two vehicles should be formed in front of the engine. In certain specified cases authorised by the Superintendent of Operation three vehicles may be propelled. In all cases the propelled vehicles must be fully fitted pull and push vehicles as described in paragraph 1 and the driving compartment must be leading.

A train may be worked as a pull and push service with the engine propelling one set and trailing one set, i.e., the engine may be formed between two pull and push sets.

When necessary additional passenger carrying vehicles or horse boxes, luggage vans, brake vans, etc., may be attached at the rear of a pull and push service, provided the hauling capacity of the engine is not exceeded and the brake regulations are observed.

(4) Electrically lighted head lamps are provided for use at the driving ends of pull and push sets. These lamps must not be used as tail lamps.

(5) When a pull and push train is run with the engine formed at the rear or in the centre, Drivers must give one short ring on the bell before opening or closing the regulator, and this bell must be acknowledged by the Fireman also giving one short ring. This does not apply to emergency stops.

(6) When a pull and push train is run with the engine at the rear or in the centre, the Guard, when provided, must ride with the Driver in the leading brake compartment, except when it is necessary for him to enter the compartments in which passengers are riding for the purpose of issuing tickets, but in any case the Guard, when provided, must be with the Driver when a train is entering a terminal station.

The following instructions must be observed in all cases where it becomes necessary for a second engine to be attached to a pull and push train :—

(7) A second engine must be attached in front, except in an emergency such as failure in a section, in which case assistance may, if more convenient, be given in the rear, in order to clear the line. This applies whether the pull and push engine is formed at the end of the train or with vehicles on each side of it.

(8) The Driver at the front of the train will be responsible for the observance of signals and the working of the continuous brake whether he is in a driving compartment or on an engine, but the Driver of the second engine is not relieved from the due observance of all signals regulating the safe working of the line and in case of need he must apply the continuous brake.

(9) In those cases where, for the purpose of clearing the line during an emergency, an assistant engine is attached at the rear, such engine must be removed to the front of the train at the first opportunity.

Pull and push train failing in double line section.—Should a pull and push train fail in the section with the engine at the rear and assistance is required from the station in advance, the Guard must obtain a Wrong Line order form from the Driver and go forward for the assisting engine, the Fireman of the pull and push train going back to protect the train in accordance with the Rules.

In the event of the engine of the pull and push train being unable to be moved for some considerable time, arrangements must be made for the assisting engine to take forward the vehicles, in which case the train must not carry a tail lamp at the rear until it has arrived at the signal box in advance, nor must the Driver of the disabled engine allow his engine to be moved until duly authorised by the Station Master or other person in charge of the traffic working. In such cases the Fireman must continue to protect the engine until he becomes aware that single line working has been established on the opposite line, when he may take up the detonators he has placed on the rail and return to the engine, or, should single line working not be necessary, until he has been recalled to the engine.

Trains assisted in emergency by pull and push trains.—Pull and push trains may be used to assist trains that have come to a stand owing to a failure, but should the pull and push train be so formed that the engine is at the rear the Driver must, upon his train coming to a stand behind the disabled train, change from the leading compartment to the engine at the rear, in order personally to handle the engine while assistance is being rendered.

Working of pull and push trains without a Guard.—A Guard will not be employed on the pull and push train working between certain places, provided the number of coaches on such train does not exceed three, and that the train is composed entirely of vehicles fitted with the vacuum brake throughout, or fully braked and piped only vehicles in the proportion authorised in the regulations for working the vacuum brake.

In all such cases the following Rules are modified as shown :—

Rules 129 (iv) and 141 (b). The Station Master, or other authorised person, must carry out the duties allocated to the Guard.

Rule 141 (e). In the event of a train being stopped by accident, or other exceptional cause, the Driver must satisfy himself that all is in order before again proceeding.

When a Porter is not travelling with such train, parcels and miscellaneous traffic must be locked in the Guard's compartment except when the train is propelled and the Driver is riding in the brake compartment where the traffic is loaded.

In the absence of a bell signal from the Driver, at those places where bell signals should be given, the Fireman must be prepared to bring the train to a stand if necessary.

PULL AND PUSH TRAINS WORKED WITHOUT A GUARD.

When pull and push trains are working without a Guard between the undermentioned points, and the engine is propelling, an exchange of bell signals, viz., two rings, must be made between the Driver and Fireman as shown :—

From	To	Point at which bell signal to be exchanged.
Plymouth Friary ...	Turnchapel	100 yards from Plymouth Friary " A " box up main to branch home, Cattewater Junc. down home, and Turnchapel down outer home signals.
Turnchapel	Plymouth Friary ...	100 yards from Cattewater Junc. up home and Plymouth Friary " B " box down outer home signals.

PLYMOUTH FRIARY TO SUTTON HARBOUR.

Name of siding.	Position.	(1) Station in Charge of working. (2) wagons labelled to †	Gradient at point of connection (1 in)	Catch points provided in sidings at.	Points of siding controlled by or worked from.	If gates provided across siding — Key to be obtained from.	Key to be returned to.	Worked by.	Remarks.
Sutton Harbour Branch	Down side Plymouth Friary	Plymouth Friary	330 rising towards Plymouth Friary	—	Hand points from goods yard	(Level Crossing) Shunter's Cabin	—	Shunting engine	For working instructions see pages 65, 66.

PLYMOUTH FRIARY TO TURNCHAPEL.

Name of siding.	Position.	(1) Station in Charge of working. (2) wagons labelled to †	Gradient at point of connection (1 in)	Catch points provided in sidings at.	Points of siding controlled by or worked from.	If gates provided across siding — Key to be obtained from.	Key to be returned to.	Worked by.	Remarks.
F. J. Moore ...	Up side Oreston	(1) Plymouth Friary (2) Oreston	Level	55 yards from main line	Ground frame. Train Tablet	—	—	Up goods services	*
Bayly's (Plymouth and Oreston Timber Company)	Down side between Oreston and Turnchapel	(1) Plymouth Friary (2) Bayly's siding, Oreston	50 falling towards Turnchapel	38 yards from main line	Ground frame. Annett's key	—	—	Various goods services	For working instructions see pages 66, 67 *
F. J. Moore Quarry	Down side Turnchapel station	(1) Plymouth Friary (2) Turnchapel	Level	42 yards from main line	Signal box	—	—	Shunting engine	Engines must not proceed beyond the catch point in the siding *
Admiralty Wharves	Turnchapel	(1) Plymouth Friary (2) Turnchapel Wharves	80 falling towards wharves	—	Extension of single line	Admiralty Authorities	—	Shunting engine	For working instructions see page 67. *

CATTEWATER BRANCH.

Name of siding.	Position.	(1) Station in Charge of working. (2) wagons labelled to †	Gradient at point of connection (1 in)	Catch points provided in sidings at.	Points of siding controlled by or worked from.	If gates provided across siding — Key to be obtained from.	Key to be returned to.	Worked by.	Remarks.
Pethick's ...	Up side between Cattewater Jct. and Cattewater	(1) Plymouth Friary (2) Cattewater	100 falling towards Cattewater Junction	—	—	—	—	—	Out of use.
English China Clay Co.	Down side between Cattewater Jct. and Cattewater	(1) Plymouth Friary (2) Cattewater	100 falling towards Cattewater Junction	Scotch block (padlocked, key held by Inspector at Cattewater)	Hand points (padlocked, key held by Inspector at Cattewater)	—	—	Shunting engine	*

Name	Location	Route	Gradient	Scotch block	Hand points	Corporation Authorities	Shunting engine	Remarks
Plymouth Corporation Wharves	Down side between Cattewater Jct. and Cattewater	(1) Plymouth Friary (2) Cattewater	Level	Scotch block, (padlocked, key held by Inspector at Cattewater)	Hand points (padlocked key held by Inspector at Cattewater)	Corporation Authorities	Shunting engine	This siding also used by Castle's Shipbreaking Co. Ltd. *
Plymouth Corporation Electric Light Works; and British Petroleum Co.	Up side between Cattewater Jct. and Cattewater	(1) Plymouth Friary (2) Cattewater	Level	Scotch block at fouling point both ends	Hand points (padlocked, key held by Inspector at Cattewater)	Two gates Inspector at Cattewater	Shunting engine	Two connections from Cattewater line, one at each end of siding. *
Lomas Gelatine Co.	Up side between Cattewater Jct. and Cattewater	(1) Plymouth Friary (2) Cattewater	Level	—	Hand points from British Petroleum Co.'s siding	—	Shunting engine	*
Passage Inn (Castle's Shipbreaking Co.)	Down side between Cattewater Jct. and Cattewater	(1) Plymouth Friary (2) Cattewater	100 falling toward Cattewater Junction	—	Hand points (padlocked, key held by Inspector at Cattewater)	Inspector at Cattewater	Shunting engine	*
Shell Mex Co.	Down side Cattedown	(1) Plymouth Friary (2) Cattewater	300 rising towards Cattewater Junction	38 yards from Cattewater line	Hand points (padlocked, key held by Inspector at Cattewater)	Shell Mex Co.	Shunting engine	*
Cattewater Loading Dock	Up side between Cattewater Jct. and Cattewater	(1) Plymouth Friary (2) Cattewater	300 rising towards Cattewater Junction	—	Hand points	—	Shunting engine	Sidings used by various firms for loading traffic
Cattedown Wharves	Down side between Cattewater Jct. and Cattewater	(1) Plymouth Friary (2) Cattewater	Level	—	Hand points	Inspector at Cattewater	Shunting engine	For working instructions see page 67. *
S.W. Tar Distilleries	Down side between Cattewater Jct. and Cattewater	(1) Plymouth Friary (2) Cattewater	Level	—	Hand points	Inspector at Cattewater	Shunting engine	For working instructions see page 68. *
Anglo-American Oil Co. and Moore	Up side between Cattewater Jct. and Cattewater	(1) Plymouth Friary (2) Cattewater	Level	—	Hand points from East siding	—	Shunting engine	For working instructions see page 68. *
Victoria Wharves	Cattewater	(1) Plymouth Friary (2) Victoria Wharves, Cattewater	Level	—	Hand points	Inspector at Cattewater	Shunting engine	For working instructions see page 68. *

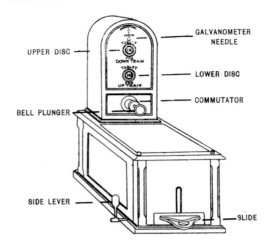

UPPER DISC

GALVANOMETER
NEEDLE

LOWER DISC

COMMUTATOR

BELL PLUNGER

SIDE LEVER

SLIDE

No. 3 Instruments.

Mode of Signalling.—" A," " B " and " C " represent three consecutive Block Signal Boxes, and the process of signalling a Train is as follows :—

Prior to the despatch of a Train from " A " the Signalman there, provided he has received the **Train Out of Section** Signal for the previous Train and permission has not been given for a Train to approach in the opposite direction, and provided the Tablet Indicators show Tablet " In," must give the prescribed **Is Line Clear** Signal.   If the Line be clear at " B " the Signalman there must, if he is prepared to receive the Train, acknowledge the Signal.   The Signalman at " A " upon receiving the repetition of the **Is Line Clear** Signal, indicating that the Signalman at " B " is prepared to accept the Train, must hold in his plunger for three seconds to allow the Signalman at " B " to lift the side lever, withdraw an empty Slide, and turn his commutator from right to left, which will change his lower Disc from " In " to " Out."   When the Signalman at " B " observes the Galvanometer Needle at zero he must hold in the plunger for three seconds, which will change the upper disc at " A " from " In " to " Out " and enable the Signalman at " A " to withdraw the Slide containing the Tablet.   The Signalman at " A " must then give one beat to " B " to denote that the Tablet is out of the Instrument.   " A " will then lower his Signals for the Train to leave, and hand the **Tablet** in the pouch to the Driver.   On the Train leaving " A " the Signalman there must send the **Train Entering Section** Signal to " B," and the Signalman at " B " must acknowledge the Signal.   " B," provided he has received the **Train Out of Section** Signal for the previous Train, and permission has not been given for a Train to approach in the opposite direction, and provided the **Tablet Indicators** show Tablet " In," must then give the prescribed **Is Line Clear** Signal to " C."

On receiving permission from " C " for the train to approach " B " may lower his Signals for the Train to proceed to " C " and hand the Tablet in the pouch to the Driver.   On arrival of the train at " B," the Signalman there will receive the Tablet (for the Section " A " to " B ") from the Driver and place it in the Slide of the Instrument ; he will then give " A " the **Train Out of Section** Signal.   " A " will acknowledge the Signal and hold in for three seconds on the last beat.   " B " will then replace the Slide and turn Commutator from left to right, which will change his lower Disc to " In " ; after he observes the Galvanometer Needle at zero he must hold in the plunger for three seconds, replacing the upper Disc at " A " to " In, "and enabling the Signalman at " A " to return his Slide to normal ; when the Galvanometer Needle at " A " has returned to zero the Signalman there will give one beat to " B " and both Instruments are again ready for use.

134

No. 6 Instruments.

Mode of Signalling.—" A," " B " and " C " represent three consecutive Block Signal Boxes, and the process of signalling a Train is as follows :—

Prior to the despatch of a Train from " A " the Signalman there, provided he has received the **Train Out of Section** Signal for the previous Train and permission has not been given for a Train to approach in the opposite direction, and provided the Tablet Indicators show Tablet " In " must give the prescribed **Is Line Clear** Signal to " B ". If the Line be clear at " B " the Signalman there must, if he is prepared to receive the Train, acknowledge the Signal and hold in his Plunger for about three seconds on the last beat. This will enable " A " to turn the Commutator to the left, and the Indication " Out " will appear on the lower Disc of his Instrument; he will then withdraw the Slide (leaving it out) and obtain the Tablet and send one beat to " B," which will change " B's " upper Disc to " Out " which " B " will acknowledge by one beat. " A " will then lower his signals for the Train to leave, and hand the Tablet in the pouch to the Driver. On the Train leaving " A " the Signalman there must send the **Train Entering Section** Signal to " B," and the Signalman at " B " must acknowledge the Signal. " B," provided he has received the **Train Out of Section** Signal for the previous Train, and permission has not been given for a Train to approach in the opposite direction, and provided the Tablet Indicator shows Tablet " In," must then give the prescribed **Is Line Clear** Signal to " C." On receiving permission from " C " for the train to approach, " B " may lower his Signals for the Train to proceed to " C " and hand the Tablet in the pouch to the Driver. On arrival of the train at " B " the Signalman must obtain the Tablet (for the Section " A " to " B ") from the Driver, lift his side lever, withdraw his empty Slide, and after inserting the Tablet in the Slide, push the Slide home, lift the side lever, withdraw the Slide empty, and again push it home. He will then give " A " the **Train Out of Section** Signal (pausing on the last beat for about three seconds to enable " A " to reverse his Commutator). " A " will turn his Commutator to the right, push his Slide home, and then acknowledge the **Train Out of Section** Signal. This will reverse the upper disc at " B " from " Out " to " In " and prove to " B " that " A " has replaced his Slide ; " B " will then give one beat to " A," which will place the lower Disc at " A " to " In " and show that both Instruments are again ready for use.

To restore a Tablet which has been withdrawn for shunting purposes (Regulation 13) or in connection with the **Cancelling** Signal (Regulation 18a), the following procedure must be followed :—

The Signalman at " A " will place the Tablet in the Slide, push the Slide home and hold it in. He will then turn the Commutator to the right, lift the side lever, withdraw the empty Slide and again push the Slide home. The **Shunting Completed—Tablet or Staff Replaced (2 pause 5)** or the **Cancelling** Signal **(3 pause 5)** as the case may be, must then be given to and acknowledged by " B." This will reverse the lower disc at " A " from " Out " to " In," and " A " will give one beat to " B " which will place the upper disc at " B " to " In."

Station and signal boxes.	Distance from next box, above. Mls. yds.	Position of box (in regard to station).	Crossover roads.		Catch points exist in		
			Position (in regard to signal box), or description.	Yards from box.	Line.	Yards from box.	Gradient rising 1 in.
PLYMOUTH FRIARY " A " BOX TO TURNCHAPEL.							
Plymouth Friary Cattewater Jct.	(From Plymouth Friary 'A') – 1,004	Up side (Plymstock side)	—				
Plymstock Station	– 956	Up side (Cattewater Jct. end)	—				
Turnchapel Station	1 77	Down side (Oreston end)	—	—	—	—	—

For particulars applicable to line between Devonport Junction and Friary Junction inclusive see instructions to S.R. staff working over G.W.R.

Station and signal boxes.	Distance from next box, above.	Position of box (in regard to station).	Position (in regard to signal box), or description.	Yards from box.	Line.	Yards from box.	Gradient rising 1 in.
Plymouth Friary " A " .. .. (To Cattewater Jct.	(From Friary Junction) – 924 – 1,004	Up side (opposite junction of Turnchapel line)	Mutley side	21	Down	655 (Mutley side)	88
" B "	– 461	Down side (Mutley end)	Down to Middle Rd. (Devonport side) (Station side) Up to Middle Road (Devonport side)	32 150 123	—	—	—

PLYMOUTH FRIARY 'A' TO TURNCHAPEL (TURNCHAPEL BRANCH)

WORKING AT ORESTON.
BAYLY'S (PLYMOUTH AND ORESTON TIMBER CO.) SIDING.

The points leading to the siding are facing for down trains. They are fitted with an Annett's lock and key, and the key is kept in the frame in Plymstock signal box, interlocked with the signals and tablet instrument, and cannot be released when a train tablet for the Plymstock-Turnchapel section is out of the instrument.

The Yard Master at Plymouth Friary will be responsible for the safe working of this siding, which will be conducted by the Guard of the train, and when any wagons have to be taken there, or brought away, the Signalman at Plymstock station will hand the Annett's key to the Driver. This key, which has a brass plate affixed to it lettered " For Bayly's siding," is the Driver's authority for proceeding on to the single line from Plymstock to Bayly's siding and no further.

The train must come to a stand at a point just on the Turnchapel side of the platform at Oreston station, before reaching the falling gradient, to enable a sufficient number of wagon brakes to be securely applied by the Guard for safely controlling the train down the falling gradients towards and into Bayly's siding. The Guard must inform the Driver the number and class of vehicles forming the train, and agree with him the number of wagon brakes it is necessary to apply in order that the train may be brought to a stand by means of the combined brake power available on any portion of the falling gradients.

The train must stop clear of the siding points where it will be met by the man in charge at Oreston who will take the key from the Driver, release the points, admit the train to the siding, relock the points and then return the key to the Driver. He will accompany the train to the Plymouth and Oreston Timber Co's yard, and when it is ready to leave there, he will obtain the key from the Driver, release the points, and after the train has passed on to the single line, re-lock the points and hand the key to the Driver as his authority for returning on the single line to Plymstock.

On the return of the train to Plymstock the Driver will return the key to the Signalman, who must replace it in the locking frame.

In foggy weather, before starting a train from Plymstock for Bayly's siding with the Annett's key, the Signalman at Plymstock must request by telephone the man in charge at Oreston to place two detonators on the rails at 100 and 110 yards respectively from Bayly's siding, on the Plymstock side, to warn the Driver that he is approaching the siding.

Under no circumstances must the Annett's key be replaced in the frame in the signal box until the train for which it was withdrawn has returned to Plymstock station clear of the section.

A brake van must always be the last vehicle of a train to or returning from the siding.

The Commission's engine is prohibited from passing the gantry which is erected alongside, and over, the loop sidings at a point opposite the premises of the Plymouth and Oreston Timber Company.

Only goods vans which are not fitted with a stove must be permitted to work over this siding, as there is insufficient clearance under the gantry referred to in the preceding paragraph for a stove pipe to pass with safety.

WORKING AT TURNCHAPEL.
ADMIRALTY WHARVES.

When a train requires to run on to the Admiralty wharves at Turnchapel, the Porter Signalman at Turnchapel must first proceed to the wharves, obtain permission from the Admiralty authorities there for it to do so, and arrange for the gates across the single line, which are situated about 200 yards from the Turnchapel station to be opened. He will then return to the station and accompany the train to the wharves, taking care that sufficient brake power is applied to safely control it.

OIL DEPOT SIDING.

These sidings which are under the supervision of the Yard Master at Plymouth Friary, are situated on the down side, and are connected with the single line leading to the Admiralty Wharves. The siding connection is worked from the Signal Box.

The gradient of the platform line, loop and single line is 1 in 80 falling from the signal box to the Admiralty Wharves and attention is directed to the requirements of Rule 151. Wagons left standing on the loop or platform line must be placed on the signal box side of the catch points in those lines. Wagons must not be allowed to stand on the single line between the catch points and the Admiralty Wharves.

Catch points are provided in the siding connection at the clearance point with the single line.

A gate, the key of which is kept in the Signal Box, is provided at the Commission's boundary.

A gate, the key of which is kept by the Oil Depot representative, is also provided at the entrance to the sidings and before vehicles are worked to or from the sidings, the Shunter or person in charge must arrange for the gate to be opened by the Oil Depot representative. After completion of the work the Shunter or person in charge must advise the Oil Depot representative that the gate can be closed and locked.

The sidings are worked by shunting engine.

The Commission's engine must not proceed into the sidings beyond the engine restriction board situated at a point 15 yards inside the gate at the entrance to the sidings.

CATTEWATER BRANCH—INSTRUCTIONS FOR WORKING.

This branch, which is connected with the Turnchapel Branch at Cattewater Junction, is worked as an ordinary shunting yard. One or more engines may be permitted on the branch at one time, as ordered by the Yard Master at Plymouth Friary, who will provide a competent Shunter to take charge of the engine at the Stop lamp referred to in the third paragraph, and remain with each engine during the time it is engaged on the branch.

Shunters must be careful to see that engines are moved cautiously, and at a low speed, from one part of the Cattewater line to another; must satisfy themselves, before allowing the trains to be moved, that the lines are clear for their passage, and must at all times keep a careful look-out for other trains, and shunting operations, and see that the several level crossings on the branch are clear.

Trains and light engines leaving this branch must be brought to a stand at the STOP lamp situated 485 yards from Cattewater Junction Signal Box, and Drivers must not proceed further until they receive permission to do so from the Inspector or Shunter in charge who must obtain the necessary authority from the Signalman by means of the telephone provided near the STOP lamp.

The box containing the telephone must be kept padlocked when not in use, the keys being held by the Inspector or Shunter in charge.

Prince Rock Level Crossing is out of use, the gates being secured across the roadway.

BLIGHT & WHITE LTD.—OPERATION OF OVERHEAD CRANE.

All trains proceeding to or from Cattedown Wharves must be brought to a stand at the Stop Boards adjacent to the premises of Messrs. Blight & White Ltd.

Before authorising the driver of the train to proceed, the Guard, Shunter or person in charge must assure himself that the employees of Messrs. Blight & White Ltd., are not operating or are about to operate their crane over the railway lines.

REGENT ASSETS CO.'S SIDING.

This Siding is connected to the Cattewater line by hand points facing for trains from the direction of Cattewater Junction. The gradient at the point of connection is 1 in 100 falling towards Cattewater Junction.

A scotch block is provided at the fouling point of the siding with the Cattewater line which must be kept locked except when it is necessary to place wagons into or remove them from the siding. The siding will be served by shunting engine from Cattewater and the Shunter in charge of the operations will be responsible for obtaining the key of the scotch block from the Inspector at Cattewater before leaving with the movement and for returning it to the Inspector after the shunting operations have been completed.

NATIONAL BENZOLE COMPANY SIDING.

This siding serves the National Benzole Company's Plymouth Depot and is connected to the Cattewater line by hand points, facing for movements from the direction of Cattewater Junction. A gate is provided at the Commission's boundary, the key of which is kept by the Inspector at Cattewater.

BETWEEN CATTEDOWN TUNNEL AND VICTORIA AND CATTEDOWN WHARVES.

Sharp curves exist on the lines between Cattedown Tunnel and Victoria and Cattedown Wharves and should it be necessary to work a bogie vehicle of any type thereover, it must not be attached to other vehicles.

CATTEWATER BRANCH.

FISONS LIMITED SIDINGS.

These sidings are connected to the Cattewater Loading Bank Siding by hand points facing for shunting movements from the direction of Cattewater Junction.

The gradient at the point of connection is 1 in 300 rising towards Cattewater Junction.

Inwards wagons must be positioned in the sidings by the Commission's shunting engine, two empty wagons under the discharge plant and two beyond. Outwards wagons will be accepted at a point immediately on the firm's side of their private roadway to which point they will be moved by the firm's capstan.

Due to the curvature of the sidings, all shunt movements must be controlled and should be carried out with the utmost care.

Under no circumstances must a wagon or wagons be loose shunted into the sidings.

Bogie stock is prohibited from entering the sidings.

ANGLO-AMERICAN OIL CO.'S AND MOORE'S SIDINGS.

The entrance to the sidings is laid on a severe right hand curve and passes across the roadway running alongside the east siding leading to Victoria Wharves and through a narrow passage cut through the rock cliff on the further side of the roadway.

At a short distance from the entrance to the siding, hand points exist leading to three separate sidings in the Anglo American Oil Company's premises, and a further set of hand points to the southernmost of these three sidings forms a connection to an intermediate siding between the southern and middle sidings. Staging exists alongside the intermediate siding for the accommodation of the Oil Company's filling plant, which staging is not of standard clearance from the near siding rail, and a notice board is exhibited near the entrance to the siding, beyond which board engines and high sided wagons must not proceed.

The middle siding extends to Messrs. F. J. Moore's lime kilns and quarries.

Shunting operations are carried out in charge of a competent man deputed by the Inspector at Cattewater.

Owing to the severe nature of the curve at the entrance to the sidings, and the difficulty of obtaining a clear view of the sidings from that point, it is necessary that movements into the sidings should be carried out with the utmost care, and the competent man in charge of shunting operations must satisfy himself before making movements into the siding that the line is clear to the point to which such operations are required to proceed.

SOUTH WESTERN TAR DISTILLERIES SIDINGS.

The main siding is connected to the Cattewater line by hand points at both ends, one facing for trains from the direction of Cattewater Junction and the other facing for trains from the direction of Victoria Wharves. A short siding which also serves the South Western Tar Distilleries' premises is connected to the main siding with hand points facing for trains from the direction of Cattewater Junction.

Level crossings, connecting the Distilleries Company's premises with the roadway fronting the Anglo-American Oil Company's Depot, extend over the main siding and Cattewater line at various points. A loading dock adjoins the Cattewater line in the vicinity of the hand points at the Victoria Wharves end.

Tractors are in use by the Distilleries Company for the purpose of hauling wagons to and from their sidings and to place wagons in position alongside and into their premises.

Employees of the Distilleries Company, before moving any wagons by means of tractors, or permitting any operations or road vehicles to pass over or foul the level crossings or commencing operations at the loading dock, must have a close understanding with the Inspector in charge at Cattewater and must keep tractors, wagons, road vehicles and operations at the loading dock, clear of the Cattewater line during the time that movements of Commission's engines and vehicles are required to be made.

Special attention is drawn to the requirements of Rules 111 and 112.

VICTORIA WHARVES SIDINGS.

These two sidings form the terminal point of the Cattewater Branch, the Commission's boundary being indicated approximately by a wall, office and weighbridge, the property of Messrs. Coast Lines Limited, who are the wharf owners.

Hand points situated approximately 100 yards on the Cattewater Junction side of the boundary, lead out of the west road of the Commission's terminal loop, and serve the east siding leading to Victoria Wharves. The west siding is an extension of the loop road.

An overhead conveyor is provided over the loop roads, at the Cattewater Junction end at Victoria Wharves, and a chute which is operated by Messrs. John Westcott Ltd., is attached to the conveyor and, when lowered, fouls both the construction and load gauges.

Before movements are made by the Commission's engine and vehicles over the right hand loop road, the Shunter in charge must obtain an assurance from Messrs. Westcott's Foreman, that the conveyor will not be set in motion over the sidings during the progress of the shunting movement.

Ingoing wagons for Victoria Wharves will usually be placed by the Commission's engine on the east siding.

Outgoing wagons will usually be accepted on the west siding immediately inside the boundary gate. The Commission's engine may proceed into the west siding for a distance of 30 yards on the right-hand loop road.

Shunting operations will be in charge of a competent man, deputed by the Inspector at Cattewater, and no movements on to the east or west sidings must be made until the competent man has satisfied himself that the line is clear and has come to an understanding with the wharf owners' employees in regard thereto.

The wharf owners' private locomotives are employed in the sidings and on the wharves for the purpose of making internal shunt movements, and such locomotives may be allowed to proceed from the west siding on to the Commission's property for a short distance towards the terminal loop, if the line is clear, up to a point where a notice board is fixed. The wharf owners' private locomotives must not proceed from the east siding on to the Commission's property beyond the boundary gate

Description of Block Signalling on Principal Running line. Dots indicate Block Posts	Stations, Signal Boxes, etc.	Distance from Signal Box next above		Running lines			Loops and Refuge Sidings		Runaway Catch Points—Spring or unworked Trailing Points			Engine Whistles s—short DOWN		UP		Remarks C—crow
		M.	Yds.	Additional UP	Principal	Additional DOWN	Description	Standage Wagons E. & V.	Line	Position	Gradient (Rising unless otherwise shown) 1 in.	Main	Relief or Goods	Main	Relief or Goods	
	LIPSON JUNCTION TO PLYMOUTH FRIARY															
	Lipson Junction ..															
	Mount Gould Junc.		814		==============				Up Main	C. 294 yards Mount Gould Junction side of Lipson Junction Up Home Signal	81					
	Plymouth Friary 'A'		1,401		==============				Down Main	C. 418 yards to rear of Down Home Signal ..	81					
	Plymouth Friary / Plymouth Friary · B ·		461		==											
	Laira Junction ..	1 0	00													
	Mount Gould Jn.		810													
	PLYMOUTH FRIARY 'A' TO TURNCHAPEL															
	Plymouth Friary 'A'					---------										
	Cattewater Junction		1,004													
	Plymstock		968													
	Turnchapel	1	77													

Electric Tablet

14

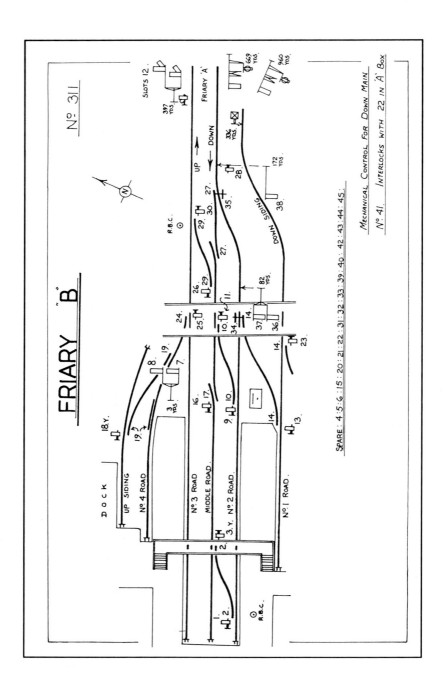

FRIARY "B"

N° 311

MECHANICAL CONTROL FOR DOWN MAIN

N° 41. INTERLOCKS WITH 22 IN 'A' BOX

SPARE: 4·5·6·15·20·21·22·31·32·33·39·40·42·43·44·45·

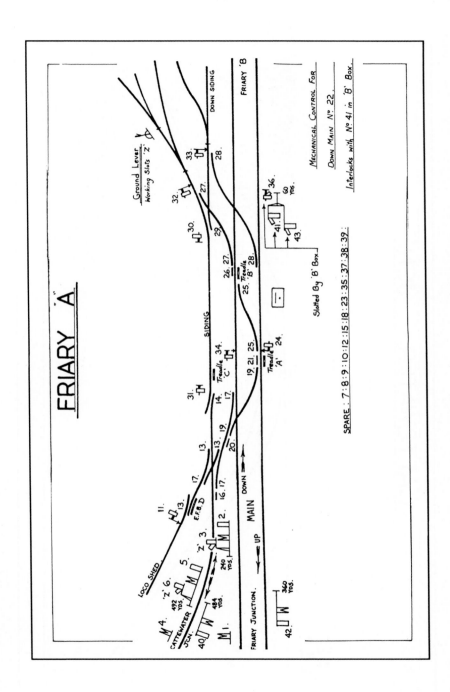

FRIARY "A"

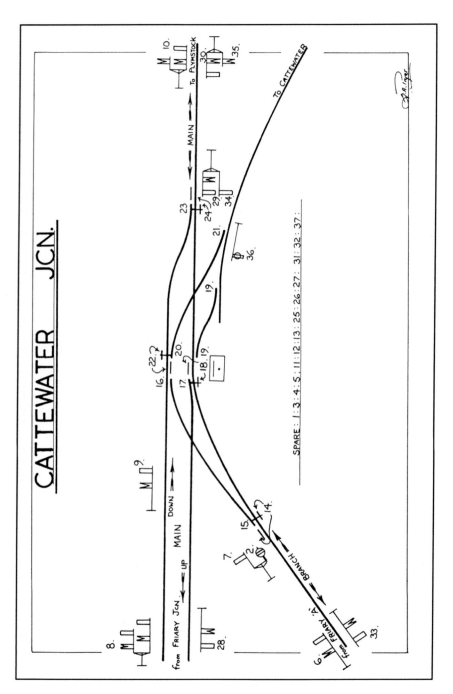

CATTEWATER JCN.

SPARE : 1 : 3 : 4 : 5 : 11 : 12 : 13 : 25 : 26 : 27 : 31 : 32 : 37 :

142

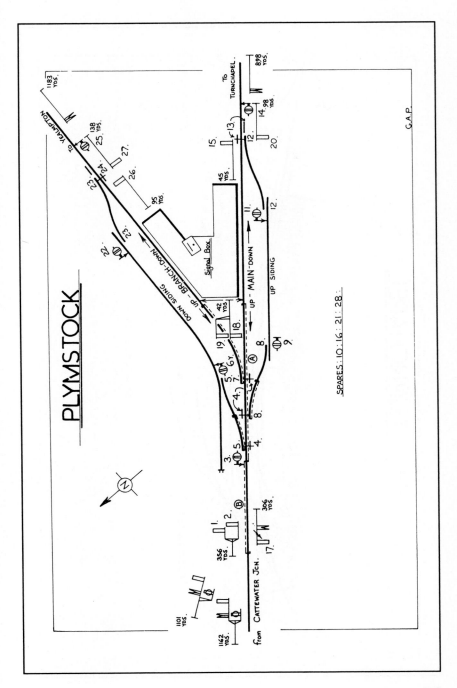

PLYMSTOCK

SPARES : 10 : 16 : 21 : 28 :

143

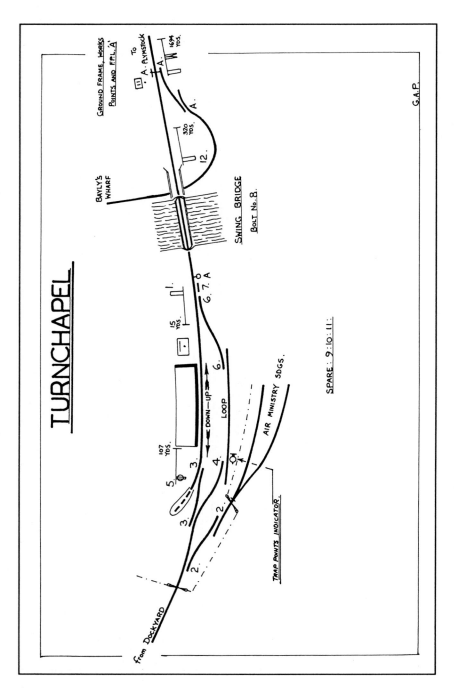

TURNCHAPEL

Ground Frame works
Points and F.P.L. "A"

To A. Aymstock

1694 yds.

Bayly's Wharf

320 yds.

12.

Swing Bridge
Bolt No. 8.

15 yds.

6. 7. A

From Dockyard

107 yds.

Down—Up

Loop

Air Ministry Sdgs.

Trap Points Indicator

Spare : 9 : 10 : 11 :

G.A.P.

LONDON AND SOUTH WESTERN RAILWAY. (941)

Indoor Goods Manager's Office, Waterloo Station, 2nd February 1921

The traffic to be invoiced as from ORESTON to FRIARY for LAIRA JCT.
and invoices to be taken to account at FRIARY separately.

We have agreed to convey a special lot of

Timber, Telegraph Poles, Creosoted Sleepers with or without Chairs, Nuts & Bolts. On account of the G.W.Co's Stores or Engineering Dept. Traffic to be loaded in G.W.Co's Stores or Engineering Dept. wagons. Haulage ONE SHILLING per ton, minimum 25 tons (INCLUSIVE of 1st SEPTEMBER 1920 INCREASES) if worked with other traffic, but no special trip to be worked

Rate and Conditions with less than 50 tons, or a charge to be paid as for 50 tons.

from ORESTON (Bayley's Siding) to G. W. Co's Siding at Laira.

To be carried before 31st DECEMBER 1921.

Agent, — J. SMEAL,

ORESTON. Station. per

NOTE.—This Rate only applies for the Special lot mentioned, and it must be recorded in a Foolscap Book open to the Public for inspection the same as the ordinary Rate Book.

SOUTHERN RAILWAY (South Western Section). (341)

Indoor Goods Manager's Office, Waterloo Station, 22nd September 192 3

The traffic to be invoiced as from ORESTON to FRIARY for LAIRA JCT.
and invoices to be taken to account at FRIARY separately.

We have agreed to convey a special lot of

Timber, Telegraph Poles, Creosoted Sleepers with or without Chairs, Nuts & Bolts. On account of the G. W. Co's. Stores or Engineering Dept. Traffic to be loaded in G. W. Co's. Stores or Engineering Dept. wagons. Haulage NINEPENCE per ton, minimum 25 tons 12 (Inclusive of 7th August 1923

Rate and Conditions increases) if worked with other traffic, but no special trip to be worked with less than 50 tons, or a charge to be paid as for 50 tons.

from ORESTON (Bayley's Siding) to G. W. Co's. Siding at LAIRA

To apply from 7th August 1923 to 30th June 1924.

Mr. Thomas,

Oreston. Station.

J. SMEAL,

per

NOTE.—This Rate only applies for the Special lot mentioned, and it must be recorded in a Foolscap Book open to the Public for inspection the same as the ordinary Rate Book.

SOUTHERN RAILWAY

PS 267

Special Rate Advice

Ref. 34/33261

Indoor Commercial Manager's Office,
London Bridge,

12th April/28   192

Advice of Exceptional Rates for a Special Lot of Traffic.

The following Exceptional Rates per ton for the conveyance of Merchandise

Operate on and from 2nd January-1928   until 30th June-1929.

Quote to the public on _____

Between	Description of Traffic.	Rate.
ORESTON(Bayly's Siding) and	The traffic to be invoiced as from ORESTON to FRIARY for Laira Junction. and invoice to be taken to account at Friary separately. Timber, Telegraph Poles, Creosoted Sleepers with or without Chairs Nuts & Bolts. On account of Great Western Company's stores or Engineering Dept.	
GREAT WESTERN COMPANY'S SIDING at LAIRA.	Traffic to be loaded in Great Western Co's Stores r Engineering Dept. Wagons. HAULAGE. TENPENCE per ton minimum 25 tons (including of 1st February 1927 increased) if worked with other traffic, but no special trip to be worked with less than 50 tons, or a charge to be paid as for 50 tons.	

B.R. 34225/1

BRITISH RAILWAYS

PN. 1/659

Western Region News

**PUBLIC RELATIONS DEPARTMENT, PADDINGTON STATION, LONDON, W.2.
PRESS SECTION, TELEPHONE PADDINGTON 7000, EXTENSION 2680/1**

No.2476   26th September, 1961

FREIGHT LINE TO CLOSE

British Railways Western Region have announced that on and from Monday, October 2nd, facilities for handling freight will be withdrawn from Oreston and Turnchapel Stations (Devon), and the line from Plymstock (exclusive) to Turnchapel closed.

This section of line is single track, $2\frac{1}{2}$ miles long, and is used by freight trains only.

Passenger trains over the branch were withdrawn in 1951.

Two views of the renewal of the original LSWR bridge over Embankment Road during November 1962. This was to strengthen the bridge in preparation for the bulk cement traffic due to commence the following year. *Top:* View from the road looking towards Plymouth. *Lower:* The Laira and Newton Abbot steam cranes lift out the second girder after 75 years of service.

Author

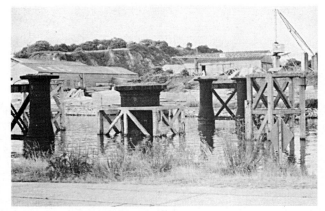

Top: Pomphlett Roundabout viewed from Plymstock Station site, looking towards the remaining abutment of Stamp's Bridge (Bridge No. 5 in the distance). March 1979.

Centre: Oreston Station site looking towards Plymstock. The track-bed is used as a public footpath. March 1979.

Bottom: The remains of the swing bridge at Hooe Lake as existing in August 1980.

Author

The now defunct tunnel under Boringdon Road, Turnchapel, viewed from the wharves in August 1980.

Author

The old bridge abutment and former entrance to Turnchapel Station as existing, August 1980.

Author

149

The truncated sidings on Turnchapel Wharves, with the Plymouth 'B' power station across the river in the background. August 1980.

Author

Mobil road tankers lined up at the Conoco oil depot on the Cattewater Branch during August 1980.

Author

APPENDIX I: SUPPLEMENTARY TRACK PLANS

The track plans contained in this appendix were recently presented to the author by Mr P. Lucas and are reproduced courtesy of the Plym Valley Railway and by kind permission of British Railways Board.

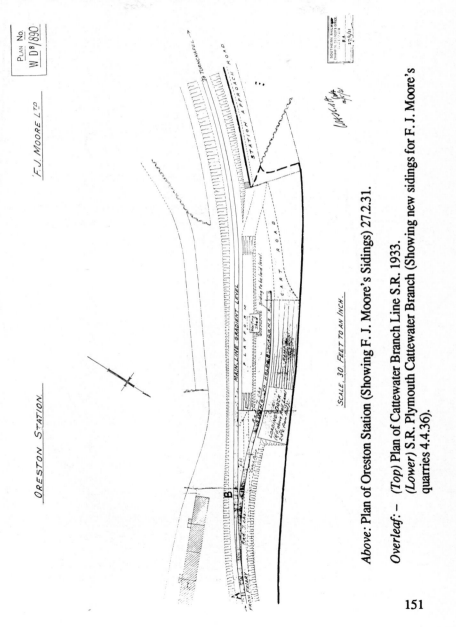

Above: Plan of Oreston Station (Showing F. J. Moore's Sidings) 27.2.31.

Overleaf: – *(Top)* Plan of Cattewater Branch Line S.R. 1933.
(Lower) S.R. Plymouth Cattewater Branch (Showing new sidings for F. J. Moore's quarries 4.4.36).

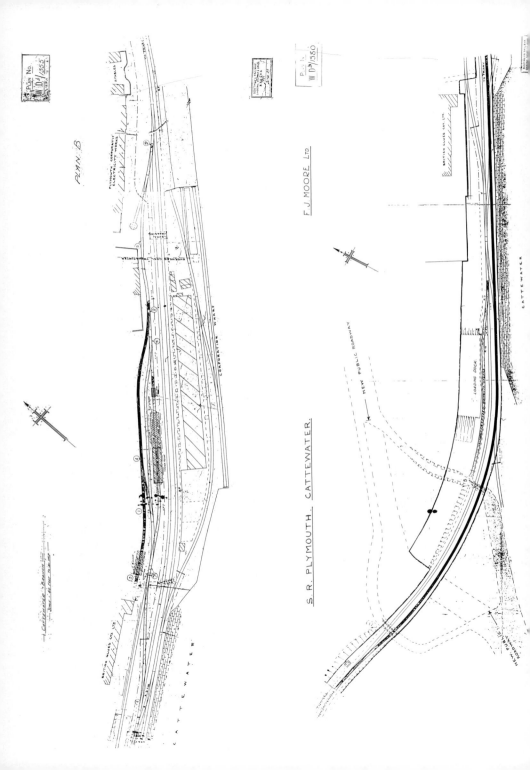

PLAN B

PLAN No.
WD⁴/1955

S.R. PLYMOUTH CATTEWATER.

F.J. MOORE LTD

CATTEWATER

CATTEWATER

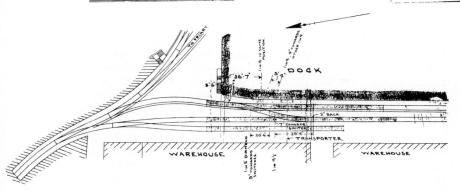

S.R. Plymouth, Victoria Wharves (Showing track renewal 2.3.31)

APPENDIX II: THE PLYMOUTH TO TURNCHAPEL RAILWAY – 1982 TO DATE

The final words of *The Turnchapel Branch* (page 72) were:- 'In 1981, only the Friary to Plymstock section remains as a siding to the cement works and liquid petroleum gas depot near to the site of the old station'.

Sadly, this has now also gone and only the forlorn and abandoned rail bridge over the River Plym remains, its only duty, as it stands victim to the elements, being to carry the 20" medium pressure gas main westwards towards Plymouth. This is, and has been for many years, secured to its northern side, and presumably British Gas SW find it cheaper to rent the bridge rather than re-route the mains via the road bridge, or to excavate a path under the river. How long this situation will remain is a matter of pure conjecture.

The bulk cement traffic of Blue Circle Industries, formerly Associated Portland Cement Manufacturers, ceased in Feburary 1987 due to the cost of rail transport compared to that of road haulage. The three rail storage depots in Devon and Cornwall, i.e. Barnstaple, Exeter and Chasewater were subsequently closed, and now all cement leaves Plymstock by road and is delivered direct to individual sites. The 'Presflos' bulk cement waggons were transferred to other Blue Circle sites where rail transport is still used.

It is interesting to record at this juncture, the generosity of Blue Circle Industries with their donations of all the rail track within their works to the South Devon Railway (formerly the Dart Valley Railway) at Buckfastleigh, and the 0–4–0 Diesel Shunter to the Plym Valley Railway at Marsh Mills. The Vanguard shunter, built by Thomas Hill (Rotherhorn) Ltd and driven by a 175 H.P. Rolls Royce engine, had been redundant since 1988: it left the cement works for the PVR on 30 March 1990, whilst the cement works sidings were lifted and sold to the SDR during 1992.

During early 1994 the rail over-bridge east of the aforementioned river bridge, and carrying the line over 'The Ride', was taken down. The embankments on either side were severely cut back, and the road into Chelston Meadow considerably widened. Plymouth City Council were assisted financially by E.C. funding for the project and took the opportunity to create a major road junction with the A379 controlled by multiple traffic lights. This facilitated much easier access to and from the Council tip and waste reclamation site at Chelston Meadow. For safety reasons the rail bridge over the river had earlier had steel railings erected across the track at each end. Pointwork branching from the Cattewater Branch was permanently locked as that line is still in operation.

This left the track east of this point and running back to the site of Plymstock Station truncated and isolated. However, it did not remain so for long, for on 7 October 1994 lifting operations began in a westwardly direction from the stop blocks situated 10 chains east of Plymstock Station site. These formed the end of 'Plymstock Siding', previously part of the former 'Yealmpton Railway' since its closure and lifting up to this point in the 1960s.

This siding was used for the storing of cement waggons after their delivery and prior to their collection by B.R. All other sidings within the boundaries of Plymstock Station serving both the cement works and the then South West Gas Board were lifted by Weaver Plant of Bristol. The very last rail of the Turnchapel and Yealmpton Railways at Plymstock was lifted at 3.50pm on Wednesday 12 October 1994, witnessed by the author. General clearance of the site continued thereafter with the recovered pointwork returned to B.R. at Laira for re-use. The remaining rail and all other fittings were removed as scrap metal, while the wooden sleepers were destined to serve a new life as fence and gate-posts on various farms after their sale.

The track-bed from the former site of Stamp's Bridge towards Hooe Lake has been converted into a pedestrian/cycle pathway to just beyond M.P. $1^3/4$, where a footpath from Broad Park Oreston crosses it; the pathway then continues towards Hooe Lake past the ruins of Radford Cottages, but the track-bed here, at the time of writing, has two wire netting fences across it, beyond which excavation debris bars the way towards the old Bayly Bartlett site. However, clues to the former railway land between this point and the former site of Turnchapel Station are contained within the pages of the March and September (1995) Newsletters of the *Radford Park and Hooe Lake Preservation Association*. This, together with the kind assistance of the Association's Secretary, has enabled me to report the following:–

The Bayly Bartlett site appears to be shared by Boston Shipping (for the purposes of running a commercial wharf, boat building, ship repairs, boat storage and as a base for marine survey work) and by Tay Homes, who had obtained permission to build 50 houses on the Hooe Lake end during 1995 but who will now be submitting revised plans following intense local opposition to layout and style.

Plymouth City Council will retain the rights to construct a footpath/cycleway from the Tay access road (from Bayly's Road, Oreston), around the edge of the lake, to the position of the former swing bridge. From that point it is hoped to construct a swing footbridge as a link across the water to Turnchapel, and Groundwork Trust has applied for Millenium Lottery funding for the project. This, in turn, was backed by the Association, who had urged the Plymouth Development Corporation that it should be part of their brief to complete the Coastal Footpath through Turnchapel to Mount Batten.

The erection of a new bridge structure will, of course, be of a much simpler construction commensurate with its new mode of traffic. The Association has long considered the bridge project as a long-standing dream, and the main obstruction has been the cost. They cautiously, and rightly, point out that it is still a proposal and not yet a certainty, but I hope that they will be successful and soon realise their dream!

Friary Station site, including the new freight concentration depot opened during 1966, itself closed and was demolished during the 1980s, and all land up to the multi-arched road bridge was sold to the Plymouth City Council for yet another shopping centre. The view from the bridge is now of a large expanse of roofs belonging mainly to 'Do it All' and 'Courts Furnishing'. New flats adorn the passenger station site and are appropriately named 'Friary Court', but these and the large stores are, from a railway point of view, too depressing to record photographically. The limestone Station-Master's house, which stood at the main entrance, has been modernised and extended to become a Health Centre.

Land to the east of the road bridge is, I assume, being prepared for sell off by 'Railtrack'. Some sidings remain, but the lure of cash is too great to retain this site for much longer; Plymouth City Council must surely have their eyes firmly affixed upon it. How sad, for with a little thought, the bridge over 'The Ride' could have been widened and Plymstock Station site turned into a 'Park & Ride' car park. Regional railways could have run shuttle services into what remains of Friary and commuters could have been transported to the City Centre. This would have resulted in cutting rush-hour traffic from the east of the city and thereby obviating any further increase of car parking facilities.

THE CATTEWATER BRANCH

The last words on the history of this line proved quite prophetic for, as far as can be ascertained, the only traffic remaining on it is bitumen. Oil for Laira Depot has transferred to the main line delivery direct from the refineries, and the LPG ceased with the closure of Breakwater Works.

The CEGB power station was subsequently demolished during the 1980s, soon after its 'mothballing', and this, and other former railway sites, have been developed extensively. Needless to say their supply and output has been wholly road traffic orientated. To this extent, a new road has been forged through the rock-face, in from the A379 – just west of the road bridge over the River Plym to join up with the various wharfs and eventually Sutton Road in the City. Its construction does, however, enable an easier route to be taken into the city, especially for the lorries supplying the light industry within this area. Yet more traffic lights control this junction, and the development, one assumes, has encouraged the closure of another City landmark, 'Follands Garage', which has stood for many years near the 'Western National Bus Depot' on the western side of the River Plym road bridge.

Further prophecy is not difficult. Once the Bitumen traffic is jettisoned by the railway as unprofitable, 'Railtrack' can then close the branch and sell off the land. I do hope I am proven wrong in this case and that privatisation will encourage MORE freight onto the railway, and in part, at least, help stem the increase in the estimated 17 million fatal casualties that 100 years of the 'car' has given to the world!

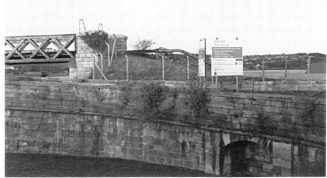

Top: The new road junction at the entrance to 'The Ride'.

Centre and Bottom: The trunkation of the Turnchapel Line east of the River Plym. The gas main and the abutment of the former 'Iron Bridge', which carried the A379 road, are both clearly visible.

Author

Top: The view looking towards bridge No. 5, showing the track-bed used as a public footpath to Oreston and Hooe Lake.

Centre: The view from bridge No. 5 looking northwards to Phomphlett Roundabout. Note the house in the centre of the picture, which replaced the former Station Master's house.

Bottom: The view from the gateway in the centre picture showing the round-about, the cement works and, far centre right, the last remaining bridge (partly hidden by trees) of the former Yealmpton railway.

Author

A demolition team from Weaver Plant of Bristol dismantling track at Plymstock Station site during early October 1994.

Author

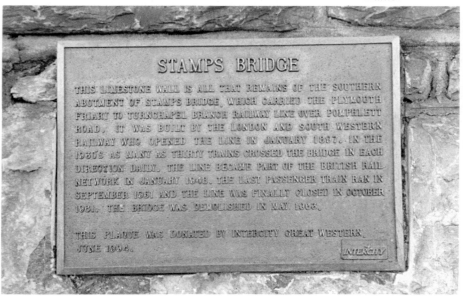

STAMPS BRIDGE

THIS LIMESTONE WALL IS ALL THAT REMAINS OF THE SOUTHERN ABUTMENT OF STAMPS BRIDGE, WHICH CARRIED THE PLYMOUTH FRIARY TO TURNCHAPEL BRANCH RAILWAY LINE OVER POMPHLETT ROAD. IT WAS BUILT BY THE LONDON AND SOUTH WESTERN RAILWAY WHO OPENED THE LINE IN JANUARY 1897. IN THE 1950'S AS MANY AS THIRTY TRAINS CROSSED THE BRIDGE IN EACH DIRECTION DAILY. THE LINE BECAME PART OF THE BRITISH RAIL NETWORK IN JANUARY 1948. THE LAST PASSENGER TRAIN RAN IN SEPTEMBER 1951 AND THE LINE WAS FINALLY CLOSED IN OCTOBER 1961. THE BRIDGE WAS DEMOLISHED IN MAY 1963.

THIS PLAQUE WAS DONATED BY INTERCITY GREAT WESTERN, JUNE 1994.

INTERCITY

Author

BIBLIOGRAPHY

A History of Western National, R. C. Anderson & G. G. A. Frankis (David & Charles, 1979)

A Regional History of the Railways of Great Britain (Vol. 1), D. St John Thomas and C. R. Clinker (Phoenix House Ltd, 1960)

History of the Southern Railway (Vols. 1 & 2), C. F. Dendy Marshall, revised by R. W. Kidner (Ian Allan, 1963)

LSWR Locomotives, A Survey 1873–1922, F. Burtt (Ian Allan, 1950)

Plymouth – 100 Years of Street Travel, R. C. Sambourne (Glasney Press, 1974)

Plymouth & SW Devon (Ward Lock & Co. Ltd.)

Plymouth Transport Centenary 1870–1970 (Plymouth Bus Club, 1970)

Southern Railway Branch Lines in the Thirties, R. W. Kidner (Oakwood Press, 1976)

The Plymouth & Dartmoor Railway, H. G. Kendall (Oakwood Press, 1968)

The Plymouth, Devonport & SW Junction Railway, A. J. Cheeseman (Oakwood Press, 1967)

The Yealmpton Branch, A. R. Kingdom (Oxford Publishing Co., 1974)

Track Layout Diagrams of the G.W.R./B.R. (W.R.), Sec. 12, R. A. Cooke

War on the Line, Bernard Darwin (Southern Railway, 1950)

THE AUTHOR

There can be few people more well known in local railway 'circles' than Tony Kingdom. Born in Plymouth in 1931, the son of the late Engr. Comdr. Charles M. S. Kingdom, himself a steam engineer with the Royal Navy from 1906 until 1934, Tony became interested in steam at a very early age and still vividly recalls 'interviews' with the driver and fireman at the start and, often again, at the completion of a train journey during the 1930's. Similarly, he also has vivid memories of trainspotting at Plymouth Laira, North Road and Mutley during the war-time years and seeing many locomotives and rolling stock 'foreign' to the area.

With the demise of the steam era in the early 1960's, Tony turned his attentions towards the field of preservation, and the many activities that followed included being Chairman of the South-West Group of the Great Western Society from 1968 until 1972 and a founder member of the Dart Valley Railway Association.

Pressure of work and the responsibilities of a young family ultimately weaned Tony away from preservation work during the early 1970's, but the vacuum was to be immediately filled by him becoming an author of Railway books. This, in turn, subsequently led to the successful publication of no less than seven titles between 1974 and 1982, while in 1990 the lack of a publisher did nothing to prevent the appearance of his eighth book: using the name ARK Publications, he published it himself!

Tony, now retired after a long career in the Post Office Engineering Dept. (now British Telecom), in which he graduated to the position of Engineering Training Manager, Westward District, currently lives in Newton Ferrers with his wife Marjorie. He has two grown-up children, Roger and Nicola, and three young grandchildren, and enjoys gardening, is a keen photographer and, during the summer months, looks forward to boating and caravanning with his wife. In addition, he likes to spend any spare time researching the history and experiences of the Second World War and, looking to the future, hopes to produce further works on Westcountry Railways as well as seeing some more of his out-of-print titles republished.

Other books by A. R. Kingdom:

The Yealmpton Branch	OPC	1974
The Railways of Devon	Bradford Barton	1974
The Great Western at the Turn of the Century	OPC	1976
The Ashburton Branch	OPC	1977
The Princetown Branch	OPC	1979
The Newton Abbot Blitz	OPC	1979
The Turnchapel Branch	OPC	1982
The Plymouth Tavistock and Launceston Railway	ARK Publications	1990
The Bombing of Newton Abbot Station (RAILWAY **ARK**IVES SERIES No. 1)	ARK Publications (Railways)	1991
The Yelverton to Princetown Railway	Forest Publishing (In Assoc. with ARK Publications)	1991
The Totnes to Ashburton Railway (and The Totnes Quay Line)	ARK Publications (Railways)	1995

The Author, photographed here with his wife Marjorie